THE
LOVE
CODES

PRAISE FOR
THE LOVE CODES

Relationships are the foundations of a stable family, community, and society, which is why learning to relate in a healthy, dynamic way is crucial for modern couples, and Belinda Bailey's *The Love Codes* is a must read for all those who desire to live a revolutionary love.

~Dr. Saida Désilets, author of *Desire* and founder of the Embodied PsychoSexual Method

Belinda's *The Love Codes* is a life changer! In her gentle and powerful way, she allows the reader to understand and experience what it is like to be trying to get love from a position of wanting, controlling, forcing to one of magnetic attraction, alignment and flow. It is very inspirational, practical and a must read for any woman in who wants deep, soul-level love.

~Amanda Leigh Walker, Lord of the Fries, age 46

This was one of the best books I have read on relationships. It is so relatable and easy to absorb the wisdom, teachings, and apply the practices. As a result, I have seen myself showing up differently with my partner, which is invaluable. Having been able to take this content and apply it practically and experience transformation, how can one not feel deep gratitude? Reading this book also concretized 'The Codes', deepening my understanding and application, after going through Belinda's Love Codes program over a year ago. Thank you for gifting us this simple, powerful framework to create relationships where we both feel seen, heard, understood and loved.

~Lisa Winneke, founder and host of The Good News Guides

Belinda is an expert in her field. I feel very blessed to have access to this work and learning the science of relationships. If you put into practice the science that this book is teaching, you can see a relationship magic playing out, inside you and around you.

If you feel like me, and especially if you feel stuck in your relationships, not sure why certain things continue to happen to you and want to have loving and fulfilling relationships; whether you are already in one or currently single, I can't recommend *The Love Codes* enough.

Not only will it help you to heal and give the gift of love to yourself, you will play an important role in sharing the gift of love with other women and men, and in that way help love to heal the world. That's why we, as wise women, are here. Come and join us.

~Petra Brzovic, therapist

THE LOVE CODES

FIVE STEPS TO AN AUTHENTIC AND EVOLUTIONARY RELATIONSHIP

For women who are ready for a soul-satisfying love

BELINDA BAILEY

Published in Australia by
Soul Center Books
Postal: PO box 294 Warrandyte Victoria 3113
Email: belle@belindabailey.com
Website: www.belindabailey.com

First published in Australia 2021
Copyright © Belinda Bailey 2021

National Library of Australia Cataloguing–in–Publication entry

 A catalogue record for this
book is available from the
National Library of Australia

ISBN: 978-0-6450091-1-8 (paperback)
ISBN: 978-0-6450091-2-5 (ebook)

Cover photography by Pauline Langmead
Cover layout and design by James Albert Silvoza

Printed by Kindle Direct Publishing

DEDICATION

I've poured my heart and soul into my path of service, which has been made possible with the dedication and love of the man who walks beside me, Warwick Johnston. This book is, in every way, dedicated to you, my love.

Your presence in my life and continued devotion to our relationship is the backbone to this work. Your unwavering faith in me is like a lighthouse; you are so loving, committed, spirited, helpful, playful, successful, intelligent, adventurous, and handsome. You are the epitome of masculine authenticity and strength, and your love for me, I cherish. You are living proof that the work I do brings real-world results, and our love inspires me to keep going.

Together we have embarked on many initiations and adventures—birthing and raising our child, moving interstate, buying a house, and overcoming health issues. Many times, through adversity, it would have been excused to shelve this project and had I been on my own, I would have had no choice. Your continued encouragement and support and unwavering belief in me and this work has been and continues to be my guiding light.

With humble dedication and purposeful action, you have provided for me and our darling son in such masterful, abundant ways, running your own successful business in the name of environmental sustainability. I am in awe of how you do it, and incredibly grateful for your generosity and strength of character.

In doubtful times I think to myself, 'Well if this man believes in me, then I must be onto something!' Your belief in me gives fuel to my fire. But most of all, I can do this type of work in the field of intimate relationships with genuine faith and reverence of the work because I have my person and I am living the depth of relationship that I encourage my clients to never lose sight of.

In my uniqueness and idiosyncratic ways, often appearing confident and able well-beyond my sensitivities and vulnerability, you see me; and in you seeing me, I've come to love and see myself more too.

Your love and acceptance of all parts of me provides me with greater confidence in all that I do.

I thank you for this gift of love and in the name of love, devotion, care, and companionship, I am so proud to be your woman and proud of the incredible life that we create together. I love you Warwick, and with the excitement of an overzealous puppy, I am excited for the years and adventures ahead for us on the horizon.

Thank you for finding me in this lifetime.

Belle x

CONTENTS

WELCOME

'Soul mate love.' The email was to my husband and the sender wasn't me.

I could hardly hear myself reading over the sound of my heartbeat. But I didn't need to read any more than the words in the subject box of the email to know that my marriage was about to end.

I don't know what it is that took a hold of me in this situation, that had me as though possessed, first reading on, with every declaration of love and detail to their ongoing intimacy like a twist of a knife in my heart. Then scrolling madly and searching furiously almost 'wanting' to find more. It's as though I wanted to find more evidence to rub salt into the wound. Or perhaps I was hoping to find something to show me it wasn't real.

Disbelief quickly turned into anger, which was being fueled by sadness and the silent, lurking driver of the behavior that followed, fear.

When my husband didn't answer his phone after me calling him at least twenty times successively. I found 'her' number. The conversation that ensued was not a high point in my career as an empowered woman of the sisterhood. And I can confidently say that the weeks, months, and years that followed were some of my lowest. I reached a place of such darkness, fear and self-loathing that I pray my journey through it and the sharing of my findings will help other women to never have to go through the same.

And I'm not talking about divorce. I'm not even talking about infidelity and the devastation it can bring. I'm talking about the years of loneliness, confusion and downright desperation of being a smart and successful, awake thirty-something year old woman who, for the life of me, couldn't get a decent date, let alone make a relationship work. Or, God forbid, have a soul satisfying connection of love with a man!

The days since that time have been many. Some longer than others. I feel I've lived a dozen lives since then.

I've been a dancer, a therapist, a metaphysical pioneer. I've lived in multiple cities and travelled many countries. I've met extraordinary and ordinary people and I've dated a lot of men. I've had long relationships, mini-relationships, and the relationships that aren't really relationships at all.

I have worked as a couple and relationship therapist and coach for more than fifteen years and started my career in Human Transformation and Potential more than twenty years ago in the field of Transpersonal Psychology and Neuro Linguistic Programming. I have since continued to deepen my passion for the human psyche and heart and how it best thrives in relationships through quantum psychology, Neural and behavioral change processes and have had the good fortune to train with some of the world's greatest minds in this space, including John Grinder, Dr Rafael Locke and, of course, the revolutionary Dr Joe Dispenza.

But I wouldn't be writing this now if I didn't eventually find all of the things that I and so many women are looking for. In hindsight, I can see that this whole experience was the fertile ground in which I was able to nurture this body of work while tending to my shattered heart and dreams.

While piecing together the remnants of my own relationship and love puzzle, I took heart in seeing it work for me and other women too. So, it is with great pleasure that I introduce to you *The Love Codes.*

I am deeply touched that you have decided to take this journey of love with me and countless other women in the pursuit of a healthy relationship, passion, sovereignty, intimacy and of course, true love.

Your participation here connects you to a vibrant community of radiant women, just like me and yourself, who have also experienced confusion, disappointment, heartache, and frustration in relationships with men, who are now enjoying true empowerment by attracting and sustaining healthy and fulfilling partnerships.

What you are about to learn will radically change the way you view yourself and men in the pursuit of love. It will comfort you with an unwavering, inner knowing that what you long for is what you deserve and is attainable. Your time has come now to relax into the reality of becoming a wise and powerful master of love and to finally step into your birthright of an evolutionary relationship.

We are going to cover a lot of in-depth information and tools, so I encourage you to journal or take notes while you read. Some insights will land right in the moment; others may take time to develop and integrate. Having your own handwritten notes will help to track your progress. You can then refer to what's most important to you or build upon new understandings along the way. You will discover things you never thought relevant on the path of love, yet these kernels of wisdom once attained, will guide you towards your heart and soul's desires. Keep those pens poised.

You'll get to know a lot about me along this journey too. I'm incredibly passionate about men and relationships, and relationships with men. I have an overflowing wealth of resources to share with you and I want to see you flourish with this new knowledge; the wisdom I have gained from years of studying, mentoring, and relating with men, women, and couples, personally and professionally.

I would like to mention that this journey is specifically targeted at heterosexual women. It is translatable to all sexual preferences, however, since my work-to-date has been with women only, my trainings are developed with heterosexual women in mind.

If you are reading this book, then you are either single and wanting to be in a relationship or in a relationship that needs some help. Perhaps you have had lots of non-starters where you go on dates, maybe you are sexually intimate (or not), and then it either goes nowhere or fizzles out fast. Maybe you are too busy to date, or never get asked out. Or you find that men are often intimidated by you; or one of the really common challenges for women like us; you meet men but they just don't seem to measure up to our perfectly justifiable standards.

Or you could be a woman in a relationship that requires some support. Maybe you are in a relationship that was wonderful, but your circumstances have changed and now you just don't see eye to eye. You don't have anything in common anymore. Maybe you find yourself no longer attracted to him and the passion has all but died, leaving you wondering if this is all there really is left for you. Perhaps you are tired of being the one to do all the work to make it work!

Or maybe you are constantly questioning if this is the right relationship for you. This can be one of the hardest situations of all, where we know that the relationship is great, he is great, but our heart just isn't in it. We don't want to leave and let go of something that is, on paper, really great but we also don't want to live anything but our absolute best life!

There are so many ways we can be confused and need support whether we are single or in a relationship, and through this journey together we will approach these situations thoroughly. What I will be sharing with you is born from research, investigation, application and most importantly a discovery of innate wisdom that you will discover within yourself that can be applicable to a variety of circumstances and situations between men and women.

Let's look at the four main types of women who will benefit from this book.

Type 1 – Terminally Single

Some of us feel like we have always been on our own and are somehow destined to a life of singledom. Deep down we feel like 'maybe, I'm just not meant to have a relationship.' This can even be the case if you have had some relationships but you may feel like those passages of time are just tiny moments between phases of solitude.

Type 2 – Frustrated Single

And then there are those of you who are convinced there is a massive shortage of single men out there or just no decent men available. You may have dates and even mini-relationships, but they don't go anywhere because the ones that are available are the bottom of the barrel, slim pickings. I personally know that feeling because I sustained that attitude for a long time, and I can attest it was very frustrating and downright disheartening. I can assure you that these are shared sentiments by many women, women who are gorgeous, talented, successful, powerful, loving, kind and truly exceptional in their own unique way, just like you.

Type 3 – The In and Out Relationship

Then of course there are those in relationships that are just not quite right, and you can't for the life of you work out if it is you, them, or simply a bad match. You don't want to leave a perfectly good relationship that many women would simply love to have but you find ourselves daydreaming about leaving and meeting the 'right' man for you.

Type 4 – Relationship Renovator

Some of you will be reading this book who are in a relationship that simply isn't working and so you feel like you are constantly trying to fix it. You read all the books, do all the courses, maybe even try weekly dates and therapy but it seems like you are doing all the work and getting nowhere.

I know how it feels to be in any one of these situations, I have been in them all at one time or another, culminating in finding myself at the bitter end of a devastating divorce that was followed by a desolate time of loneliness and confusion. I found myself suddenly single in my thirties and suffered a desperate lack of quality men in my life, yearning for intimacy and a meaningful, valuable connection, I felt trapped and very isolated in my experience of love.

Even though it is in my character to always push on towards a better outcome for myself, that little voice of reinvention and possibility was very quiet this time and it wasn't until I had trodden down the path of self-pity for long enough that I had almost given up when I heard it squeak its little voice. No doubt this voice had been screaming at me for months, but I had spiraled so far down the path of fear and loneliness that it took another wake-up call to get me to actually listen.

I had the good fortune, finally, of having a sweet dalliance with a lovely young man, the very first one since the divorce, but it wasn't going so well. He was running hot and cold, and with my very low sense of relationship self-esteem it was pushing me a little closer to the edge.

On one of these mornings where I was balancing dangerously close to this edge, I went to a local brunch with some girlfriends who had all been 'Terminally Single' for a long time. And after listening to them all for a while it truly dawned on me that I really was heading down the same path, in fact I was *speeding* down the path I had always feared. The path of being forty-something, single, bitter and no possibility of having a family.

It was as though someone had slapped me in the face and taken my breath away. I had been wallowing in this sense of failure and doom as though it had already happened, and in this rare—at the time—lucid moment, I saw that this meant I was *allowing* it to happen.

And while I had been allowing myself time to heal my heart, which was genuinely necessary, in this moment, I saw how it had started to slide into self-pity. That little inner voice that told me that although I was just the same as all these other women, I had one singular difference: I had so many more tools than they did. Therefore, for me, there was really no excuse to keep hurtling down that track. With more than twenty-five years of experience working within the field of human potential and specifically with women in relationships, what was I doing just obediently accepting my unwanted fate?

I went home and sat on my bed, looking around at all the reminders of my failed marriage and I thought about Ash, the guy I had been seeing, and I sat upright, held my head high and asked myself the question. 'Belle, do you really want to love and be loved again?' The answer was that I was terrified. That little inner voice spoke up and told me there is a way and that we will find it together. It also told me that I had two choices and only one would lead to finding true love and a healthy relationship. I could keep my heart closed or, beyond my own comfortability, I could force it to stay open.

Until this point, since my husband left me, everything within me had told me to stay safe, to avoid being hurt further and to be smart this time! But in this moment, I knew that the only answer was to keep my heart open. To do this meant that I was willingly opening myself to potential further heartache and pain. It meant I had to be 'vulnerable' and in hindsight I now know that this is precisely what it means to be vulnerable, that the word 'vulnerable' in itself means 'willing to be wounded', as was shared with me many years later by the wonderful Transpersonal and Jungian therapist and dear friend, Jeremiah Abrams.

It was indeed in this moment that my much wiser inner-self was telling me that if I wanted to learn how to love and be loved, I needed to keep my heart open and be willing to be wounded.

My response was 'Ok, But! Only if I can be safe too. Only

if I can find the algorithm, the patterns to healthy attraction and relationships.' After all, I had all of the training and intel to do so. My inner self and I shook on it. I knew I had hit the sweet spot with how to move forward because my body—for the first time in ages—felt relaxed, and I could see the faint beginnings of a pathway forward. Even though it felt a little like a well-meaning crowbar was prying open a tightly closed space in my chest!

It became clear to me that my years of training in Transpersonal Psychology, and the many years working with couples and women to build healthy models of relating had been in pursuit of this moment. The moment for me to finally become the person I wanted to be, in the relationship that I wanted to be in, and along the way to build this body of work to share with you.

It really has been an astounding journey for me of learning the deeper, intrinsic and quantum capacity for a truly evolved model of love and relationship, and it has been a great gift to share this with my clients and friends who are repeatedly having profoundly healing and successful outcomes.

Wherever you are in your own relationship journey, whether you are Terminally Single, Frustrated Single, or in a Relationship that is In and Out or a Renovator, we all want the same thing: to love and be loved in a way that we know in our bones that we are in the right relationship. And the energy that we receive from the relationship far outweighs the individual energy we put in. We all want to feel desired and pursued when we are single, and the desire for desire remains when we are in a couple. *The Love Codes* lays out the bones for how we can create this for ourselves, regardless of where you are in your relationship status right now. This is because the Codes are something we apply to ourselves, and the external world will respond without any mention of it to another soul. That is because the Love Codes will give you a foundational understanding and training in Relationship and Love skills.

I have been very humbled to have helped hundreds of women over the world to meet their life partner. Or to turn their rapidly declining partnership around into a union of true love and connection. I am confident this book will help you too.

LOVE CHRONICLE #1

Lisa came to me when her marriage was dissolving. She had a burning desire for a deeply connected relationship in her future. Lisa journeyed through a myriad of potential relationships and finally, through this work, met her now partner who is nothing like who she thought he would be. I'll always and forever remember the moment where she truly cracked open her heart of hearts with him. They had been having a really hard time. She felt like he just wasn't being who she needed him to be. She wasn't feeling heard. And in one moment, when the three of us sat together and applied a simple yet effective Love Codes tool, it was as if a veil lifted. The love that flowed between the two of them in that moment was nothing short of a miracle that I was honored to witness. And the best part is, that it was a turning point from which they never went back. She herself will tell you till this day how deeply loved and met she now is from this man.

It is exciting to say that I have discovered the pattern and formula behind why some women repeatedly attract high quality, loving men who commit and keep stepping up into their lives and why others do not.

I am humbled and, honestly, relieved to be able to announce that these years of drudging through my own heartache and applying all of my wonderings and curiosities to myself first and then finding the same success repeated time and time again with my dear friends and clients, that I have—with the help of so many women opening up and sharing their own journey and trusting me to help them through it—finally discovered a repeatable formula in how to have a real and soulful relationship.

I want to share with you that we have been tricked and hoodwinked into believing that it is supposed to be hard, that we aren't good enough, that the men aren't good enough or that love is a battlefield. I am beyond grateful to be able to confidently say that! Relationships are supposed to be joyful and fulfilling and we are here to enjoy loving and being loved. It is part of our reason for being here and our birth-right as a human being.

And it is with the passion of my own desire coupled with the desire of women all over the globe to finally live this destiny that I have cracked the Love Code, and I want nothing more than for you to benefit from my findings.

I have developed and delivered my programs to many women around the world, all of whom have integrated these new Codes and transformed their experience of relationships for the better.

This book is your entry into the Love Codes and can be viewed as a sacred transmission that clearly you are ready and waiting for.

Allow me to walk you through this map, to guide you home to your heart of hearts...

1

WHY THE LIST DOESN'T WORK

Let's talk about The List.

You know the one, where you list all the things you desire in a man? It's the running sheet to the dream; the toilet roll list to Mr. Right. You fervently knock it into shape, redraft and refine it after the last failed relationship with a zero-point focus and unwavering conviction to settle for nothing less—and quite possibly have it reviewed and qualified by a trusted girlfriend for reinforced execution!

You vow that the next guy will be different, and The List is there to remind you to hold the vision (as it tends to slip your mind when you fall madly in love). You've written this list or perhaps re-written it again as you realize that this last man really wasn't that much different to the previous one. He, too, didn't listen to you, the passion died out, you submitted to being controlled. The sex was lousy, or any other manner of patterns that we have. But! Now you have The List and you will never fall back into the trap!

But we do...

Many women swear by their List and while there is nothing obviously wrong with it, or getting clear and conscious about what you are calling into your life, my question stands:

Why hasn't The List worked?

And it hasn't, because if it had, you wouldn't be reading this book. You would be in your very happy and healthy relationship.

There is a reason The List doesn't work, and this reason is a huge part of the puzzle as to how to find and keep love in your life. To begin, I will help you build a framework of understanding on which to base this essential information so that you can move with confidence past hopeful list-making into a place of truly being able to attract all that you desire.

To create lasting and ecological change, it is essential to understand the building blocks of our psyche and psychology. And it is essential that the changes we make are ecological to our entire life and internal value structure. Because if we make a change in the area of our love life that is not in alignment with another area of our life, we may find we have fleeting success in love. Yet once it trickles down into other areas of our life, if it is out of alignment with our overall value structure then the changes will simply unravel. It is like having a garden where we wish to grow both flowers and fruit—it is important to give both types of plants that which they need. If we start to focus only on the flowers and what they need then we will have wonderful flowers, but the very thing that feeds the flowers may be poison to the fruit, and the fruit perishes. Within our psyche as a whole system, if we make a change that is good for one area of our life but not another, the unconscious mind will simply eliminate the most recent change. Putting you right back at square one.

In order for us to be able to create ecological and therefore lasting change, we need to understand the difference between the conscious and the unconscious mind and specifically, how these two parts of yourself play a huge role in your love life.

THE CONSCIOUS/ UNCONSCIOUS INTERFACE

The conscious mind is the part of our mind that we are, quite simply, conscious of. It's the thoughts, beliefs, and feelings that we are aware of having at any given moment. In basic terms, it is all the things you know you know.

The unconscious mind is the part of you that is choosing all the hidden potentials and possibilities that you are completely unaware of, and yes, there are always hidden possibilities and aspects of our behavior of which we are unaware. For instance, what is it that makes me choose to speak to a particular person at a party or to avoid someone at a party? What is it that has me choose to lose my temper with my son or to be calm and let it go when he accidently rips my scarf? These are things we do not choose consciously; to do so would take up so much of our headspace, and we would never get anything of importance done. So the unconscious mind is constantly choosing which pathway to lead you down. It makes these choices based on many things, including past experiences, cultural narratives, and our beliefs regardless of if they are healthy beliefs or not!

When you draft your list, you are using your conscious mind to make decisions about what you want, as well as to articulate what you consciously desire. And this is good, this is part of the job of the conscious mind: to determine where you want to go next.

While this is happening, the unconscious mind is playing a huge role behind the scenes—it is looking for opportunities as to HOW that desire could be created in your life. When the conscious mind is doing its job and the unconscious mind is doing its job and they are working in harmony with each other, we have a healthy conscious and unconscious interface.

The inner workings between the conscious and unconscious mind is not a new concept, and probably not new to you either. It has been thoroughly explored throughout history and was first made popular through Jungian psychology.

The issues begin when we realize that the unconscious mind is not discerning when it comes to what we say or think we want. This means, that whatever we tell ourselves to be true, the unconscious will find ways to manifest it. This is true for our helpful and not so helpful thoughts. And so when we tell ourselves that we want to have a happy relationship, but we have a strong, underlying belief that we are not worthy, the unconscious mind, like a dutiful drone will simply go about finding ways to manifest that belief. That we are unworthy.

And as most of our limiting beliefs are entirely unconscious to us, meaning we don't know that we have them, we find ourselves continually in the same old, destructive, unsatisfying situations and relationships.

Until we can make this process conscious by bringing to awareness what those limiting beliefs are, we will always end up with the same results. The really tricky part to discovering these blockages and changing them is that not only are they unconscious to us but they are almost always linked to real experiences that have us convinced that this destructive belief is true. For instance, I used to have an unconscious belief that I am not worthy. When I finally unearthed this little sucker, I also discovered that it originated from an experience of being told that I am a bad and evil person and when people find this out, they will not like me. Yeah, I know a real doozy right!? But the point is, this really happened, so convincing myself that I am worthy—when as a child I was told time and time again that I wasn't—is no easy feat. Hence, the work of the Love Codes.

This all means that no matter what you say you want, no matter what you write down on your 'list', what you will get is being controlled by often destructive thoughts that you have no idea about!

The important issue here is that no matter how clever you are, your unconscious is and always will be outside your awareness. This explains that no matter how hard you try to consciously make a change, it will always be sabotaged by unconscious patterns and behaviors until you are able to detect and transform them.

THE POISON BLURT PROCESS

As discussed earlier, it is our unconscious limiting beliefs that were usually formed from a young age in relation to our experiences and stored in our unconscious as a fact. It is this that now holds you back from having your ideal relationship.

Just like what happened to me when, as a child, I was told that I was evil. I believed this to be true and decided that being evil meant I would not have and was not worthy of love. I mean how could an evil person be worthy of love?! This belief is then stored in the unconscious mind as a fact.

The reason we just take it on as fact and don't question this belief is because most of our beliefs are formed in the first seven years of our life when we have not developed the ability to discern and dissect information. We are in fact existing mostly in a brain-wave state known as Theta, which is the same state we enter when hypnotized. So as you can imagine, whatever we are led to believe in these formative years, lays the foundation of our beliefs about our self and the world. And this information is stored in the unconscious. It needs to be, because there are so many things for us to learn and remember about life just to survive, that if we had to be consciously aware of them all, we would have no headspace for anything else.

The really good news is that we do know now that our neural pathways are malleable, and we have access to tried and tested tools such as various neural plasticity processes that will enable us to reorganize our habituated pathways and change systemic belief patterns.

The Poison Blurt process is one such neuro plasticity process that will powerfully change your destructive unconscious beliefs around relationship and provide you with a lifeline out of the old and into a new, upgraded way to be in a relationship. In a moment, I will invite you to imagine your ideal relationship, and it is important when doing this to not hold back! I want you to imagine the kind of relationship you really, truly want. The no-holds-barred relationship. The absolute biggest dream. The one that you may have even stopped believing could ever come true or could never figure out how to manifest.

Most of us started off with a grand vision of what we want to have, and over time have played it down to something more 'realistic' which is then reflected in our thoughts about it. 'I would be happy with even something a little less than perfect,' we tell ourselves.

But today I encourage you to imagine the type of relationship that you *truly* desire.

Through this process, I will ask you to visualize something and then take note of the intrusive, negative thoughts or Poison Blurts that pop in. As soon as you hear a Poison Blurt, please open your eyes, write it down and then as promptly as you can, close your eyes and resume the imagining. It's important to accept that we all have a destructive and negative voice that is attached to our unconscious limiting beliefs and it is this voice we are looking to listen to. It can be a challenge at first as we have spent decades learning how to ignore it. So be patient with yourself, you will hear it. The more you hear of what it is saying, the better chance you have of finally changing your experience in love.

The best way to do this practice by far is to go to my website (link below), and you will be able to listen to me take you through the process. This is the best way to free up your conscious mind so that you can truly access those destructive beliefs. Alternatively, you can record yourself speaking the instructions and then listen to yourself while you do it.

It is also fine to read the instructions as you go but this will be a much less effective way to complete the process.

https://belindabailey.com.au/the-love-codes-resources/

The Poison Blurt Process

With your eyes closed, please take a moment to visualize your ideal relationship. Let yourself really go there. See yourself and see The Man. You might see what he looks like and you might not; that isn't important. It's enough just to sense his presence. Take time to really imagine what it's like to be together and playfully imagine what you might be doing. And give yourself the time to sink into and enjoy this reality.

As you start to amplify your images and dreams, pay specific attention to that little voice inside you that starts commentating with negative thoughts.

These are called Poison Blurts. I want you to hear what that voice has to say, and when you catch a blurt, write it down.

Promptly jot it out in its simplest form then gently return to the dream (with closed eyes). Stay inwardly focused. As you return to your vision, allow yourself to be completely open to your dream relationship. Pay attention to what is happening and keep listening for that niggling, interruptive voice.

Take your time to capture these blurts and return to your inner world. Keep stoking the dream. If you really want to change your circumstances, then you really must give this your all. What have you got to lose? Notice exactly what makes this relationship so fulfilling. What kind of things are you doing together? What kind of things do you say to each other? Are you travelling? Getting married? Are you creating an empire together? Keep paying attention to that voice trying to derail the entire love affair.

It will be commenting on your storyboard and may well be unkind, diminishing, or cruel. Don't worry, write the Poison

Blurts down. The more of these statements you are able to write down, the more chance you have of finally changing the unconscious processes that keep you from having the relationship you really want.

We all have a destructive, inner voice. It is worth using this practice to gain full awareness of it. What is yours saying?

It's not true.

You can't have that.

You're not worthy.

You don't deserve it.

You're too fat, ugly, or old.

It's too late.

Listen to that voice.

This is really important. As you imagine that dream, what does that negative little voice inside you say?

It's too much.

You're too much.

Men are intimidated by you.

Men can't be trusted.

They only want you as a friend.

This is ridiculous.

What is it saying to you?

Write it all down, and once you write down one little blurt, return to closing your eyes and delve deeper into your imagination.

You will find that the longer you do this, the more you will hear. Listen to that voice. What else does it have to say to you?

We spend so much time and energy ignoring it so this may be slightly challenging to bring it to the fore. But trust me, it does exist for all of us. It's important for you to hear it, and once we've acknowledged it, we will re-program it.

Keep pumping up the dreams! Turn them right up!

Give yourself one more minute of limitless dreaming and if there's one last Poison Blurt hidden there, capture it and write it down.

Now open your eyes and stay in the present moment. Well done!

This is why The List fails you. It doesn't matter how much you say with your conscious mind or how much you yearn for what you want in a relationship, this programming—these Poison Blurts—lurk in the unconscious mind and are the thing that actually drives what you get out of life. It is this voice that is determining your future outcomes. And if you look at what that voice is saying, it is little wonder that relationships are not working out for you and for most of the women we know.

You see, the unconscious is programmed to prove itself right. It doesn't discriminate between right and wrong or good and bad. Its only concern is to prove your beliefs and your unconscious programs, to be right. This means it will seek out situations that give you the experience of your belief being true.

Now chose one of the Poison Blurts and ask yourself:

'Is it any wonder that I am not getting anywhere in love when I am programmed to find THIS?!'

Let's say that one of your blurts is that 'men are not interested in commitment.' Your unconscious will seek out situations to support that belief. It does this by way of focus. To put quantum science simply—as so effortlessly explained by Dr Joe Dispenza—we know that all potentials and possibilities exist at once, and it is only by putting attention on something that it comes into being. To put this a different way: all possibilities exist and are in reach, and your unconscious mind will be a radar to elicit the life experience that matches your unconscious beliefs.

What we do know through modern quantum physics, is that all matter, all 'things' have a 'frequency' and in the quantum field or unmanifest paradigm, frequency attracts like frequency. This means that our unconscious thoughts and feelings have a particular frequency, and they draw to them experiences of a similar frequency. So despite the fact you are writing The List, you continue to find yourself in relationships that are destructive or unfulfilling or don't last long at all. Because it is the thoughts and feelings or 'programs' beyond your conscious awareness that are the 'magnet' for your experience.

Did you know that your unconscious mind is much more wily and encompassing than the conscious mind? If your conscious mind is everything that you know that you know—as in *everything*—then the unconscious is all the things you have no idea that you know, such as how to digest food, how to grow skin cells and all your unknown, conditioned beliefs. Of all the things that you know, the conscious mind makes up only 5% of your mind. This means an astounding 95% of your mind is unconscious!

If your unconscious mind is saying all these nasty things to you about relationships—these destructive, negative, poison blurts—your unconscious mind is what drives you forward in life. We know that it is, because as discussed in the previous chapter, it is the job of the unconscious to, without judgment, find situations to prove and manifest your unconscious beliefs to be true. Whatever you've got hidden away in your unconscious mind is what you're going to be silently and invisibly pulled towards.

The Pole Story

This concept reminds me of a story I heard about a particular stretch of road in the south-west of the USA. It stretches for thousands of miles without passing anything significant. There are virtually no signs of community and the road is very straight. The only noticeable things are the telegraph poles punctuating the highway.

It is surprising to hear that along this particular stretch of road an abnormal number of accidents occur against these poles. The number of motorists who swerve off the road and head straight into the posts for no apparent reason, is unbelievable. This led to the authorities being suspicious of what was actually happening, and to look further into the phenomena. They discovered that drivers are not under the influence, which gave rise to enquiring further into why people were so vulnerable to having accidents on this particularly non-descript road.

What they discovered proves my point about the unconscious mind—that it will always direct you towards whatever you are focusing on, or whatever is latent in the unconscious mind, no matter how you consciously try and avoid it. They discovered that the common factor in all these motorists was that they were aware of these poles and aware that they needed to steer clear of them on a conscious level but as they were driving for long stretches, eventually they would veer right into the one and only thing they were unconsciously aware of on the road. The poles.

As they were driving and not seeing much else, they were aware at the back of their mind of these poles—the only thing they were aware of after some time—so they were drawn directly into them. This is tragic but true!

So, whatever is lurking in your unconscious mind, I can assure you, backed by decades of research, that it will profoundly influence what you create in your life. The time has come to clear those cobwebs and you can start by doing the Neuro Plasticity List exercise.

What I will be providing next is a new map for the journey, accompanied by some exceptional tools and the Initial Love Codes that will instantly bury that old list and qualify, quite effortlessly, that where you are heading is towards your heart's wildest dreams where all those Poison Blurts are long dead and buried.

Chapter Highlights

- ♥ The List: what it is and how it *doesn't* serve you.

- ♥ How to recognize your unconscious belief patterns at play.

- ♥ How to change these patterns so they align with your dreams using the Neuro plasticity, Poison Blurts Exercise.

- ♥ Conscious/unconscious interface.

2

HOW INTIMATE RELATIONSHIPS CREATE FUTURE HAPPINESS

Let's look at why relationships are so important to us—that they are not purely about indulging in romance or passionate love affairs. We explore the deeper role they play in our long-term wellbeing and why we are intrinsically compelled to create them.

I've been in the human potential and transformation industry for more than twenty years. My work with individuals and couples world-wide has continuously revealed that the most popular driver relative to happiness is intimate relationships.

And it's not surprising. Did you know that statistically people in relationships are happier? A survey conducted by the London School of Economics with 200,000 participants[1] indicated that people in relationships are generally happier.

---

1   www.lse.ac.uk/News/Latest-news-from-LSE/2016/12-December-2016-1/
     Relationships-and-happinesslAJS1

Perhaps it is your own discontent with being single that compels you to do this work, that you'd be more at peace when settled in the right relationship. If you consider all the people that you know who are single, you may have also observed that most of them spend a lot of time and energy desiring intimacy.

We naturally gravitate towards relationships. The fact that you are taking the steps to inquire further as to why you haven't yet attracted a sustainable, loving relationship, reveals that this is true for you too. On a deep soul level, you believe a healthy partnership will increase your satisfaction in life and you are prepared to nurture and cherish the right relationship and do the transformational work in order to attract one or transform the one that you are in.

Sometimes this deeply known but uncomfortable truth about relationship and happiness is the very thing that gets in our own way of making the change. Sometimes, when single, we are not willing to really accept or admit that we really do want to be in a relationship. We are tired of feeling like there is something 'wrong with us' for being single. We are tired of feeling like a third wheel, for feeling judged, and feeling like we need to 'explain' ourselves for not having a partner. We want both—to be in a relationship, and to know we are very valuable and worthy as our own individual single self too! It creates quite the dichotomy.

This is all a hang-over from an antiquated, patriarchal system that is thankfully on its way out. A social and cultural system that had men at the top of the hierarchy and women way down at the bottom, which meant women had no standing, voice or say in the society or their own life without a man by their side. In the eyes of society if you didn't have a man, you were no one. I know that we are all pretty glad to be seeing the back end of that one!

However, it is this old paradigm and the wounding it has sustained that is partly responsible for our reluctancy to admit that we would dearly love to have a happy relationship.

It has left many of us angry and defensive about the fact that, 'yes, we do want to be in a loving relationship' because it conjures up the wound of being told that we are nothing without it. Yet, denying what we genuinely want is a huge roadblock to learning how to have it.

One of my favorite ways to circumnavigate this issue is instead of rebelling against this ridiculous projection that you are nothing without a man by saying you don't need or want one, is to admit you are worthy of all things just as you are. AND you really want to be in a loving relationship. An 'evolutionary' relationship, a relationship that has evolved long past that old paradigm, one that continues to evolve and is therefore evolutionary.

We want this, not because we are nothing without a man but because we are so very much that we absolutely want to share that with someone. We are part of the relationship revolution, where being in a loving relationship is our way to heal the world.

Often when we carry past hurts, trauma or even stigma around the association of binding happiness to relationships, we tend to reject this area of our life entirely. Not you, not anymore. That you have taken this step with courage and an open mind, with the right guidance, persistence and commitment to change, you can make the relationship of your dreams a reality. You *can* do something about it, and you are, which demonstrates to me the right kind of attitude when facing any conscious or unconscious obstacles that stand in your way.

Next to health, relationships are the most important thing in the world

I always say to my clients that, next to health, relationships are the most important thing in the world. While it's a big statement to make, I wholeheartedly believe it to be true. We only need to stop and think about what it is that we spend most of our time and energy on. What is it that we speak with our girlfriends about most of the time? What is it that movies are made about? Songs are written about? If we are to look at where we as humans invest most of our time and energy, it is abundantly clear that relationships are it. And if relationships are that important, if they take up that much space in our own minds and command the majority of our society's focus then why wouldn't we invest time to learn how to do them well? If they are the thing that is proven to provide us with the most happiness, the thing that all people are focused on in their final hours, then why wouldn't we pour our hearts and souls into learning how to make them great?

This force compelling you to invest yourself into making these changes indicates that it's of the utmost importance to you too.

Since I started refining my expertise in this area, the connection between personal development and relationship skills has gained strength and momentum throughout our popular culture, which is a very positive trend. It is becoming more acceptable for people to talk about intimacy and actively focus on developing skills in this area—something that previously has had a lack of role modelling and resources available. I am honored to be part of this growing movement and thrilled to see how the Love Codes have a role to play in propelling the evolution of relationships forward, and it is the recognition of this growing movement that leads me to think about Sue and Anousheh.

LOVE CHRONICLE #2

Sue started her career as a general counsellor and was naturally drawn to and passionate about working with asylum seekers.

One of her first assignments was to work with a middle-aged woman called Anousheh, who was from Afghanistan. This woman had been through so much heartache and tragedy. She was forced to leave her home and everyone that she knew and loved. Many of her family members and friends had been murdered, and for Anousheh to save her own life, she had to bravely venture to Australia—a country she had never been to. She had no belongings, no money nor personal connections and there was no guarantee she'd even make it there alive. Can you imagine?

When Sue started working with Anousheh, she had been through all this tumult and yet was simply grateful to be alive. The grief and trauma she carried was palpable, but Anousheh continued showing up to her counselling sessions like a pillar of strength. It was only after a handful of sessions that she revealed to Sue that she had something she felt uncomfortable to share, something Sue assumed was relative to the sensitive information she harbored around the traumatic experiences endured as a refugee.

Not so! Anousheh confided that she had met a man and was having feelings for him, but she was conflicted as to what to do out of respect for the family she left behind. Anousheh was genuinely distressed over these matters of the heart and was seeking guidance.

This issue, compared to the impact of leaving one's own country under duress, may seem relatively insignificant, however for Anousheh, it had become the most pressing subject of her counselling sessions. The potential of forging a new relationship and exploring love had propelled itself to the fore! And this is no coincidence given what research has proven. That regardless of what is going on in our lives, if matters of the heart reveal themselves to be addressed, then it quickly becomes center stage of our psyche. This instance truly illustrates how pertinent and valuable the roles of relationships play, and that investing in this area of your life is certain to positively influence your future happiness. If this was the most important thing even for Anousheh to speak about, after all that she had gone through then it is ok and healthy for you to want, and place precious time and energy, helping it to manifest for you too.

MY STORY:
DIVORCED AND DATELESS
TO SWEPT OFF MY FEET

My childhood history set the tone for a lot of distortion and toxicity growing up. I lived in a difficult home with frequent arguments. Although our relationship has since been healed, my memories of childhood are tainted by this hardship, as well as my desperate attempts to try and effect some positive change.

My father was a policeman and without us really knowing it, was suffering from Post-Traumatic Stress Disorder. He covered it well behind his fun loving and goofy personality but the shocking reality he faced day to day, and the horrific violence he was exposed to took its toll. And there were the many days that he wouldn't handle it very well. As children I don't think we were aware of the extent of this hardship on him and also especially on my mum and their marriage.

My mum wasn't very happy back then. She was living the life she was expected to live and playing the good-girl part. And seeing me being my free-spirited self really triggered in her the unrealized aspects of her own true nature. This propelled her to feel deeply frustrated with me and at a loss for what to do as she too was an, as yet, unrealised free spirit too. This put a strain on our relationship.

At the same time as this caused me to feel confused, I always knew that my parents did their best, and their behavior was only ever a result of their own past experiences.

I am also certain that this very difficult time is what led me to develop an early interest in relationships. I grew determined to find ways to 'work things out' rather than resort to harmful behaviors. I yearned for everyone to get along and for there to be harmony. I really do want to add here the deepest gratitude to my parents. Who are no longer married and on their own journey. My father who is taking courageous steps to overcome his own turmoil and my mother who has since taken the time and courage to heal this relationship with her inner self and with me and we now enjoy a healthy and loving connection.

Due to this desire to create more positive ways of relating, my early experiences with men were actually very good. With positive intentions in motion I attracted great quality boyfriends right up into my twenties. Young men were pursuing me and desiring commitment, often in contrast to my girlfriends who weren't having such luck. I wasn't the prettiest girl on the block, but my attitude was magnetic, and I was having positive experiences. I didn't think much of it at the time until my depth of insight about relationships began to form and mature from experience.

When I was twenty-one, I met a man and fell madly in love. Eventually we got married and I was convinced that I was going to live happily ever after. The Dream. In the bag!

I was completely wrong.

It wasn't the dream at all. It became a nightmare. Abuse crept back into my world and the supposed 'man of my dreams' was unfaithful. I learned that after ten years of being together, he was having an affair. He blamed me for this, and I believed him! I was, at the time, a very confident woman but I soon lost all confidence and self-esteem in a tower-crumbling moment as I watched my marriage dissolve. It became clear to me that even strong, capable women could find themselves in these situations. I became a total wreck of a person.

Eventually he left me. I was absolutely devastated. Not only because it was the end of my marriage and sense of self but because I thought the dream of lifelong partnership that I cherished had now slipped through my fingertips. It's hard to express the depth of depression and grief I experienced at this time. To say I was utterly shattered is a gross understatement. I struggled to face each day, and often just didn't. I cried every day for a very long time and a lot of the time, it felt like someone was sitting on my chest and I couldn't even breathe.

Before the breakdown of my marriage, I recall having nightmares of suddenly being single and alone in my thirties. I had a deeply held fear of this ever happening. To me, this was the image of failure in the eyes of society. Too old to find love let alone forge a family with a beautiful man. And then here I was, I had awoken to the living reality of my greatest fear—I *was* that frantic and desperate woman who was on the look-out for a good man, and quick!

As soon as I was able to think of anything other than my pain and grief, I instantly turned to frantically wanting and trying to find a replacement man. It became my obsession. I felt my ovaries pulsate like radars every time a man walked by. I scared myself with such strong reactions, but I couldn't control them. This continued for a long time. I was single and experiencing what many women do—that dismal feeling that there are no decent men around. I wasn't meeting any of quality, and I certainly wasn't being asked out by them. The few men that did show interest were far from desirable.

Eventually I reached a tipping point. I wasn't coping with my situation compounded by all the limiting beliefs I was carrying. I was well aware of my sorrowful state and the disempowered funk into which I had descended. Yet there was a turning point and I'll always remember with deep gratitude this fated day.

A friend of mine called out-of-the-blue inviting me to meet her at our local café—a hub of activity where we always bumped into other friends we knew. I dragged myself and my depth of depression down to meet her in my daggy track-pants. No bra, unkempt hair, the classic 'Not Coping' look. I just had to get out of the house and be with a friend despite having no energy to care for little else.

I rocked up as a bit of a wreck; however, my dear friends didn't bat an eyelid and embraced me wholeheartedly. I observed myself from the outside, almost as though in a trance, sitting at the table with my girlfriends with one foot in their world and the other seemingly off the planet. They were immersed in their usual topic of conversation—men—and I felt removed from the conversation in my own despairing bubble, just sitting back and taking in the surreal nature of the scene.

Most of these friends had been single for quite a long time and the conversation revolved around their experiences with men and why things hadn't worked out. 'He never called back' and 'don't worry, men are freaks,' 'men never know what they want,' and 'they are scared to commit' all echoed through a tunnel of detached observation. 'Did you see Augie? I think he's single again' and 'Check out how much weight I've lost!' The usual, giddy conversation of women's voices kept looping around me. I furrowed my brow and withdrew into my chair, and just like that, like a cold slap in the face, I realized I had become the very thing I was afraid of—I had become *that* woman.

In this epiphanic moment I coyly reeled further into my seat and the world came to a slow-motion halt. It was a defining moment in the history of Belinda and her path of self-realization, that if I didn't do something about this now it WAS going to be too late and I would lose my opportunity to make my dreams a reality: my dream for true love and devoted partnership with a man who deeply loved and cherished me.

It took time and dedicated personal development, but I did grab the reins from that moment onwards and steer my life not just back on track, but towards my heart's desires. As things started to turn around for me, I wondered why on Earth didn't I do something earlier? And I also wondered with a slightly heavy heart, how things may have been different in my marriage had I made these discoveries years earlier.

I began to unearth answers to the unintentionally single-life dilemma I had created, and occasionally kicked myself for not recognizing these clues sooner. Fortunately, I was in a position as a relationship specialist with lots of tools, resources, and mentors in the field as well as my already present and now rapidly growing interest in relationships to extend my knowledge and apply new modalities to my personal situation adding this to decades of training in pattern detection and transformation processes. I was on a roll now, connecting the dots and pooling everything together. All of my experience working with women and their relationships over the years came to the fore and the information I'd gathered from my own history with men presented patterns of behavior from which I could track and learn.

I started to look more deeply at the women who modelled

positive relationships with men and for whom it seemed effortless to attract quality men into their lives and draw comparisons with others who couldn't find a decent catch at all. The results from all my findings were life-changing! I started to apply these to my own life and quite suddenly I started attracting men. It was as though everywhere I went— even in the most unlikely places—men were taking an interest in me. I wasn't shortening my skirts or refining my flirtation skills, I was simply being myself yet possessed with a stronger sense of self and embodied wisdom. Men were naturally drawn to do things for me, to genuinely get to know me and take me out. It was truly nothing short of amazing and a complete turnaround from my not-too-distant dark nights of the soul.

As I reflected on the change and pondered what had made it so, it became apparent to me that there was an element to my success that seemed unusual; something I hadn't quite considered before but I knew was essential to the massive inner-shift that had taken place and magnetized men to me. That as a result of all the inner-work I had done, men were pursuing me, and this became an integral part to my eventual success within relationships. In the following chapters, I will share with you how this and more can all come about for you too.

There I was, surrounded by men, having fun and, admittedly, playfully enjoying this atmosphere of going on dates, adventures, and flirtatious escapades with more than one man at a time. I had shifted from feeling alone and devastated to suddenly being surrounded by men who were desiring me, pursuing me for dates and practically lining up to take me out. And they were decent, attractive, quality men leading purposeful, healthy lives.

It was profound and super exciting and led me to believe I was on to something. So I began to share my discoveries with friends and clients to see if they, too, would get results. It was beginning to work for everyone!

After quite some time of reveling in the fun and enjoying the fruits of my labor it became apparent that even though I was having a ball, not one of my connections was going that next step. This had been fine up until the time I began to crave deeper intimacy and soulful connection. But I had no idea how to make this quantum leap. A long-term relationship was something I was yearning and felt ready for. I wanted commitment but how to turn these wonderful affairs into meaningful long-term commitment?

I turned back to the work.

I revisited exploring patterns of behavior and the psyche of women who seemed to effortlessly not just *attract* commitment from men but *inspire* it. When I applied what I was learning to the men I was dating, they almost immediately stepped up to the plate. A couple dropped off the map, which, far from being a worry, was part of my success story as it supplied me with an effortless filtration process that became a foundation to one of the Love Codes as it provided me a clear way to know, in my bones, if someone was a worthy match. Others pursued me further and expressed their desires to take our relationship to a whole new level.

Can you imagine? Having the ability to inspire a man to *want* to give you all that you want in a relationship? Without 'asking for it'? It's truly powerful. And it was then that the Love Codes started to really reveal themselves to me.

I started to see how each step of the way there was a very specific process, and this led me to shift my focus onto two specific men that I had developed stronger feelings for and desired to go deeper with. Who up until now did not want a committed relationship.

One of these men, Jonah, was a very handsome, slightly younger man who was successful in his academic career. He was an excellent dancer, and we had the most incredible chemistry! He was very attracted to me too and was clear that he wanted to date me and treated me with real care and kindness. However, he wasn't ready to 'settle down'. At the time this was fine with me as I was also exploring and enjoying circular dating (where you date multiple men at once). But when I felt the pull toward wanting to have a deeper and more stable commitment with someone, he was one of the men on my radar.

The other man that came to the forefront of my heart at this stage was another beautiful, fun, and very deep man, Peter. He ran a successful creative company across three countries. We had met initially overseas but he had been to Australia to see me and he had flown me to at least two other continents to be with him. Although we were both seeing other people, when we were together it was as though no one else existed. Our connection was a trifecta—head, heart and soul—and we had been having an earth-shaking love affair but he was adamant he wouldn't settle with one woman in one country. He was very committed to not being committed!

Neither of these men were ready for a commitment and I had been happy with that, until I wasn't. Which is when I started to apply the foundations of the Commitment Creating Code and neural pattern changes within myself. At which time they both changed their tune dramatically.

At the first was Jonah who, without fanfare or even mentioning his previous boundaries of non-commitment, asked if I would be interested in looking at some land with him, with the vision of building a home and starting a family together!

Followed very closely by Peter who called me from France. I'll always remember this because I was sitting in the back yard of a home I was house sitting with a friend of mine and when the phone rang, I just knew it was him. My heart beat so loud that I could feel it in my throat, and I turned to my friend and said, 'Oh, my God, I think it's Peter and he is going to ask me to marry him!'

Well, he didn't ask me to marry him, but he did say that he had realized that we made the perfect couple and although he hadn't wanted to be with only one woman in the past, he could now see that this is what he really wanted with me. He then went on to explain that he had put the wheels in motion to see if he could permanently be positioned in Australia so that we could be together. And asked if I would, otherwise, be interested in living full time in one of his residences in Europe... Yah, melt!

This is the kind of life that I had always wanted but in my heart was too scared to admit, because after years of heartache, I didn't want to be disappointed. At an age in my life that is supposed to be hard to find a partner, I was being offered all that I wanted. The Codes were true, and this was really working!

And not just for me. I was sharing these Codes with friends and clients who had been terminally single for years-on-end or in non-committal relationships and they, too, were getting ground-breaking results. I still to this day recall the most significant moment for me when I realized that I was dwelling in my happiness again and had recovered my dream of The Dream. My faith had been restored and life experience was revealing this to me. I was living proof that regardless of your love-life situation, it can be turned full-circle and the most desired dreams you cherish in your heart can become long-term realities.

Now imagine what it would feel like to reclaim your dreams that may have been torn, tossed about and wounded upon the journey of love and romance. Begin to feel confident in the knowing that this is attainable for you; that you can and will have it. That residing in this place of trust and inner knowing is the best place to be to attract it into your life. Remembering, maybe for the first time, that you are enough, you are worthy, you are deserving of everything you desire. You just need the map.

Even though all I wanted was a healthy and committed relationship, I was admittedly a bit gun-shy. I'd been married before and it didn't work out. I was unable to jump straight in with a 'yes' for either of these men. I knew that I had to make a wise choice this time, so I gifted myself with a sacred pause in the process. I waited and applied the Love Codes to making this choice too.

Two weeks later I met yet another man that I had never known existed, yet I knew I would meet. I was flying to Byron Bay for a much-needed break from Melbourne. I knew that as soon as I landed, I would have an online meeting that I needed to take within an office. So a friend of mine informed me there was a spare office where he worked, and his boss was happy to hire it out by the hour. When I retired to bed that night, I had this feeling in my bones, the hair on the back of my neck stood up and my heart swelled with love. I knew that I would meet a man the next day. I was so sure of it that I even wore nice clothes on the plane. This may seem like an insignificant detail to some, but my girlfriends will attest to the fact that I always wear the most unattractive and comfortable clothes when flying. It has been a point of much hilarity amongst my friends who mostly don't want to sit next to me when flying because I look like I should be at home watching Netflix on my own! But not this time.

The next day, I dressed well but I didn't really think about it again.

My friend picked me up from the airport and took me straight to the office and introduced me to his boss. And um, I think he had to pick my jaw up off the ground. He was a 10/10! He was handsome with that very masculine-looking face and muscular surfer physique. Clearly a sharp mind, which to me is an immediate aphrodisiac, his one liners and hilarious quips had me in the palm of his hand from the get-go. But his fluffy little puppy that he had at the office and the fact that his business was focused around saving the planet sealed the deal. I was smitten!

He made it very obvious that he was interested. I remember I went into my little office and started the Skype call (ancient times before Zoom) and I was in the middle of my call when he just knocks and enters, with the puppy. I played it cool, to him, but to the person I was speaking with, not so much (sorry Ally). As soon as he entered, I hung up the conversation with not so much as an explanation. Ah, I was so taken aback by his masculine presence and his very confident and forward approach.

He asked if I would like to take the dog for a walk with him (swoon), to which I replied, I would love to but had back-to-back sessions.

Later that day, just before he left for home, he came in and laid it all on the line. He told me that I intrigued him, that he knew I wasn't around for long and he would like to get to know me better, so could he take me out.

Um, let me think about that for a minute... YES!

So, I did what any self-respecting, long-term single woman would do—serious background research, Face-stalked him, rummaged through his online public photos bike-touring Europe and hanging with friends at festivals. Pored over photos of him with his father and with nieces in his lap, playing with kids and delivering public speeches on the fly. I felt just a tad excited to discover this man who seemingly had so much going for him: a successful career, a good relationship with his dad and with children, well-travelled as well as being able to have fun and let loose. I decided it was pertinent to ask my friends to assist with further research. Did anyone know him and know more about him? Which they did.

I learned that he'd recently come out of a marriage and that he wasn't interested in commitment. He was more up for 'playing around,' to heal his heart and explore the world. My heart sank upon hearing this update, but I decided to give him a go anyway. What the heck! I had other men wanting to be with me and it could just turn out to be a bit of fun, to spend some time getting to know one another. Besides, it was an opportunity to apply my newfound way in a relationship and test out the Love Codes in a low-risk relationship.

We went out on a date. I was pretty nervous but remained calm. I felt confident that the first Love Code—*Attractive Persuasion*—was well in place (and it didn't damage my confidence that I went to this date straight from another one). We enjoyed each other's company. At first, we just went for a beach walk. We talked about everything; nothing was off the table. I rambled and he listened. We went so deep on that first date it was as though we had known each other forever. He held my hand, it was so romantic, and he laughed at my jokes and the conversation just rolled on effortlessly which for me, who connects through conversation, was a big turn on. There was chemistry and it was very sweet and innocent, no kissing just hand holding. But I wanted more! Thankfully, we made it back to his place where he asked if I would like to continue the date and go for dinner. There was such chemistry, and I was feeling blissful and inspired and I loved that he didn't kiss me still.

He took me for a delicious meal with my favorite cocktails and then he asked, 'So I guess I should ask you, what is it that you're looking for?' And I thought to myself, this was it. I thought he was going to give me the whole I'm-not-looking-for-a-relationship talk that I'd heard a million times before. Having heard it from so many men in the past, I had perfected my response with fabulous ambiguity so as to avoid getting hurt, to something along the lines of, 'I don't know... perhaps a bit of fun and see where it goes.' When really, deep down, I was ready for commitment and I was very attracted to this man in more than one way.

So this time, I was not only able but was compelled to be honest, even though I had heard he didn't want the same. I told him that I wasn't looking to play around and that I wanted something more solid and committed. I had to be honest.

'Well,' he said, 'this is the time I would normally say that I am not looking for anything long-term myself, but I have to say, you are blowing me away and I can see that you're not the kind of woman that a man should pass over. I want to take things further with you.'

Butterflies cascaded through my heart. He leant in and kissed me. My happiness shot through the roof.

It didn't end there though. After this date he pursued me and made it very clear that he wanted me. He rang every day and about a week after our first date, as we lived in different states, he organized to fly me out to see him every ten days for the next three months.

And all of this from the man who didn't want to commit.

Our second date lasted three days. We started discussing about wanting to live in the same state and would I be willing to move and where did I want to take this? He basically laid his heart bare on the table. It was and is quite literally my dreams come true. And it wasn't just me lapping up all this love—other women applying the Love Codes were getting outstanding results too. A revolution was rising.

As for my relationship with this man, there was a lot more to come. More on that later...

LOVE CHRONICLE #3

Like I said, it wasn't just me, there were other women having the same results. Just like one of my clients, Gillian, who came to see me because she was tired of feeling frustrated and disappointed over her non-eventful love life. She was thirty-seven and had been divorced for two years. She had been dating a guy for just over a year and was developing strong feelings for him. The only problem was that he didn't want a commitment even though they had a positive emotional, intellectual, and physical connection. But he wouldn't take her out in public. They only ever spent time together at his house. He wouldn't introduce her to his friends, and he wouldn't meet any of hers. She sensed the circumstances were less than ideal for her, but she kept telling herself that the connection was strong enough to override these issues.

I know many women have been in this situation before and told themselves the exact same reframe—overlaying the reality of a man with a potential or ideal framework to convince ourselves it's good enough. I have been there myself and even though we are all intelligent enough to not fall for this trap, we do. It is very seductive because <u>it's</u> true—the special connection exists—however, other potential red flags can lurk in the shadows.

Gillian came to me and I walked her through the Love Codes. She quickly applied Code 2—Invisible Influence—to her situation. Now remember, Gillian desired marriage with children; the entire white-picket-fence dream. This was very real for her and this man had always known this but was adamant it would never be his desire.

A month later he called her up and said, 'I'm ready for it. I want to do this.' And the funny thing is, upon hearing this from him she said, 'I don't know. I don't know if I do anymore!' This surprised them both.

He said, 'Maybe you don't understand. I want the whole thing. I want to get married. I want to have kids.'

She was, of course, blown away. Everything she had been wanting from him was now being offered to her.

There is more to her story and Gillian did end up getting the whole package in the end but for now it's enough for you to know just how simple changes and tools applied were able to turn her whole experience around in this relationship.

Perhaps you can tell I'm excited about this and that I love sharing this work with women. This is because I trust the process and I'm committed to seeing it through with you. I know that there are many offerings out there that promise you the keys to intimate relationships; however, what stands out about this work is that it's not about manipulation techniques. You are not being asked to do or be anything that is unnatural to you. You will not need to compromise your own essence, your character, your own unique way.

The Love Codes is a map—a guided journey into unlocking your own innate relationship wisdom. It will aid you in uncovering what is already alive yet dormant inside of you. That's why so many women, when they come across my work, say 'Of course!' as though they knew it all along and have simply needed to be reminded. It is innate to being a woman and being your beautiful self with an enhanced set of Codes to set your love life to align with your desires.

Each one of you reading this already possesses this relationship wisdom and when you unlock it you will attract quality men. You will be capable of maintaining healthy and loving relationships, the way you know relationships are supposed to be: harmonious, joyful, unconditionally loving and anchored in trust.

And this is why I am so passionately committed to seeing the journey through with you and helping women become more of their true self, and to fulfil their life purpose through their most intimate relationships. My personal mission is to create positive change in the world through human potential and transformation specifically through creating positive, evolutionary relationships. I help people to love and to be loved. I wholeheartedly believe that we can heal the world by living healthy, vibrant, affirming relationships and that this revolution needs to start with us modern women. By affirming the value of our feminine approach to love and guiding our men and relationships back to a place of healthy and happy inter-relational love.

I'm not the only one committed to this cause. In 2009 at the Vancouver Peace Summit, the Dalai Lama announced that,

'The world will be saved by the Western woman.' Whether you are Buddhist, Catholic or a die-hard atheist, I think we can all agree that this is a profoundly wise, self-realized and intelligent man and I do believe that what he says can be translated into loving action. A healthy, loving relationship is one of our most powerful tools to help realize this.

By creating fulfilling, loving and healthy relationships through unearthing our innate relationship wisdom to attract and nurture true love and partnership, we are affecting powerful positive change for our communities and the entire planet at large.

I can't emphasize enough, that I have completed this work myself and worked with women all over the world from all walks of life with all kinds of relationship situations. Many of these women, just like you, have moved on from shattering heartbreak, betrayal, and complete loss of faith in love relationships, to discovering their dreams turning to reality.

I've personally witnessed the women through my program start attracting quality men, to enjoying dating again *and* have a choice of with whom they'd like to deepen a relationship with. I've seen this so much that I've had clients *complain* to me that they are genuinely struggling with who to choose. I'm not kidding! I've seen women move through my program who were on the brink of divorce, transform their current relationship into a deeply fulfilling and soul satisfying marriage. I've celebrated these women falling in love with men who are deserving of their love and finally, get to create that mutual sanctuary to evolve into a relationship where the woman is feeling truly seen, met, and held for who she is.

And, so now, finally, it is my privilege to walk with you through this map and home to your heart of hearts. There is a wealth of information to cover so keep those pens poised to record the nuggets of wisdom that resonate strongly with your journey. You will want to reference your insights and track your progress on this rich and rewarding path of self-discovery. It is my honor to walk alongside you while you graciously trust in the next steps of true love unfolding. Let's do this!

THE MAP

In this section I outline the format of *The Love Codes*. You will be introduced to the foundation of the work, the Codes and the new paradigm of relating that will unfold as a result of applying these Love Codes. Which will be further unpacked in the following chapters.

Quantum Relationship Foundation

To begin, we must consider a new paradigm of relating; a fresh approach to operating in a relationship. Envisage the terrain of your intimate landscape with a man like a map, based on strong foundations. This is the basis of a healthy and natural relationship intended to exist outside old programs and patterns that previously may have held you back in a separatist experience of relating. When this foundation is locked in place within the coming chapters, we open to a deeper, more authentic and fulfilling relationship. An 'Evolutionary' relationship.

Upon this baseline we introduce five Codes that form the interlocking web of this new paradigm. Even though this approach is innate and natural, we have a multitude of conditioning to overcome and heal, and these Codes serve as gateways into an entirely new experience free from suffering, addiction, and the baggage of past experiences.

Code 1: Attractive Persuasion

This code explores and engages your ability to attract that which you truly desire.

Rather than repeatedly enacting relationship cycles and

patterns, Attractive Persuasion reinforces that your reality becomes a true reflection of your soul's desires. Code 1 will have you surrounded by quality men who are attracted to you and who are actively pursuing you. If you are already in a relationship, once you embody Attractive Persuasion you will find your partner changes his behaviors willingly. More specifically, he will begin to 'step up' to meet you in his masculine strength.

Code 2: Invisible Influence

The Code of Invisible Influence puts you in a position where men are willingly choosing to provide you with what you want. This is a beautiful and compassionate Code to unlock that assists the men around you to evolve into the type of man they really want to be. Applying the art of Invisible Influence is one of the more profound and satisfying relationship skills that nourishes and supports both men and women on a soul level.

Code 3: Heartbreak No More

This is a highly effective and valuable process of learning to make wise choices so that you are always getting closer to your relationship goal without being derailed by men who, at first glance, appear to be the dream but end up walking you down the garden path. With Code 3—Heartbreak No More—you gain the power of true discernment and the capacity to be moving towards your relationship goal even while seemingly standing still. With this in place your love life never loses momentum.

Code 4: Layered Vulnerability

Vulnerability is a hot topic in relationships. Being vulnerable and able to trust are essential in cultivating soul-quenching relationships that are devotional and honest, where you feel unconditionally loved, cherished, and accepted for who you are in truth and at all times. Layered Vulnerability steps you through the process of trusting while remaining empowered in your most delicate of vulnerable expressions, and I teach you how to weave this through the ever-evolving trance of falling in love.

Code 5: Evolutionary Sex

Once we've activated the Codes, we get to immerse ourselves in the delight of sex and the profound connection it brings. An extremely popular part of this work, Evolutionary Sex is an alchemizing Code that naturally unfolds once all other Codes are embodied and flourishing.

It is no secret for the modern-day woman that we enjoy sex. For those who are in a sexual relationship, we fervently yearn for sexual connection that runs soul deep. We desire world-rocking, ego-dissolving love-making that results in a merging of you, as Divine Woman, with the essence of a Divine Man. I believe this kind of sex is our birth-right and available for every woman to experience, regardless of the 'type' of relationship you're in.

I've kept the process simple. We will be looking at each of these areas in much more detail and unpacking how they play-out in relationships. You will begin to understand them, integrate them, and unlock their powers as transformational resources. Once these are activated in your reality, there will be no turning back. These Codes will define the script of your future relating.

Before we begin it is helpful to position yourself on the spectrum of your love life, in terms of where exactly you sit in relation to your end goal. There are actually many phases on the journey to love; experiences and attitudes we go through within ourselves and towards men that are common among women. I will explain them to you so that you can pinpoint where you are at on the journey towards your Evolutionary Relationship, and from that point can do the necessary work alongside integrating the new Love Codes.

Chapter Highlights

♥ We acknowledged that intimate relationships contribute to our overall happiness and wellbeing.

♥ By looking at my personal story, it is evident that transformation of your love life can happen if you are willing to make changes and do the inner work.

♥ We now have The Map and an outline of the five Love Codes that we will unpack in the coming chapter, which will permanently redefine how you relate with men.

3

THE LOVE LIFE SPECTRUM

There are many common experiences women have in their love lives, and through my vast experience with women and relationships, I have been able to identify key areas we may all go through at different times. In this chapter I describe what these areas are, so you can pinpoint where you are at on your own journey and be comforted in the knowing that the issues you are exploring are a natural part of the process.

LOVE LIFE FRUSTRATIONS

There are two types of frustration that single women have with men. The first is when you meet a man and they are undeniably interested in you. They make that clear in their behavior so you begin to sense that they would like to deepen the connection. Yet it soon becomes apparent that they can't admit this to themselves or they aren't capable of directing the relationship towards something more. They run hot and cold or from hot *to* cold. Everything suggests to you that they want more but they are unable to admit it.

The second type is those who would love to have that frustration because your actual frustration is that you can't seem to meet a decent man! There either hasn't been anything of quality around or no one has lit your fire. You have not been pursued in seemingly *forever* and there's an illusion that all the 'good ones' are taken.

For women in relationships, one of the most common frustrations is that it started off wonderfully then over time, he seems to have taken a back seat in the relationship, leaving seemingly everything up to you. Not putting in much effort and certainly not embodying his masculine energy.

What I want to assure you is that if you are dealing with any of these frustrations, know that it is not your fault.

I have discovered time and again, that it is not a woman's fault and any inkling of blaming or sabotaging yourself in response to these frustrations is completely unwarranted. Just as we discovered in the previous chapters on limiting beliefs, these are the culprits for these frustrations and if it wasn't for the history of past experiences that have impacted your psyche, heart, and soul with tremendous betrayal, hurt and distortion when it comes to love, then the belief that it is unsafe to love or that you are undeserving of the kind of loving relationship you dream of would not be running the show here and hence, blocking you from experiencing your ideal relationship.

The culture of our society has a massive influence here; that it's not acceptable for you to be in your naturalness as a woman.

That you must be more practical and logical in matters of the heart and productive and directive in all that you do. That mind-sets such as creativity, collaborating and receptivity are nice so long as they don't get in the way of real life. If it wasn't for this narrative imposed by our culture that an empowered woman must be productive and rational in every way, then I guarantee there would not be such manifold blocks in the way of true love. You would, instead, be effortlessly attracting men, and men would be jumping at the chance to enter a commitment with you. Because I can assure you—men want that too. What you yearn for and desire in a fulfilling, loving relationship based on mutual respect, honor and true love... they want that too.

It's ironic that I'm now writing a book about women and relationships, intimacy and conscious relating. I've been down the road of 'workshopping' my love life many times. Attending seminars, signing up for tools and roadmaps. A lot of the time I felt as though I was being told to be someone's slave lady, that I needed to bow to men in order to win their affection. Other times it felt as though all the women in the room were there simply to confirm to each-other that men really are the root of all evil or an elusive creature that requires stealth manipulation in order to 'pin down.'

None of that applies here. I won't be teaching you how to manipulate men and I certainly won't be talking about how to catch a man. I won't waste your time telling you how to act, dress or talk in any other way than what comes naturally to you. Nor will I be introducing complex spiritual systems whereby you need to wear orange for ten days then bury a rose upside down in a fairy garden upon which you chant mantras. I won't be doing any of that.

Instead I will empower you with some revolutionary wisdom that is central to a healthy and dynamic relationship that will resonate so deeply with you that you will wonder how you had not known it before. And the pinnacle of this wisdom is that...

Every man has an unconscious and primal need that can only be fulfilled by a woman – and it's not sex.

I'll say it again. *Every man has an unconscious and primal need that can only be fulfilled by a woman*. This is transformational knowledge that will form the foundation of your love life from this point onwards.

The way in which a woman fulfils this need is born from her innate wisdom and power as a woman. It may be untapped in you for now but when you unlock this for yourself, you will be compelling. Men will be magnetically drawn towards you. It elicits a primal instinct that urges them towards you, and no, it's not sex driven. However, men being unaware of the root need for this in their life will often mistake this for wanting sex.

Before I reveal this intrinsic truth, I want to explain to you the different levels of relationship on the Love Life Spectrum so that you can get some clarity on where you are at on the journey yourself.

You may relate to at least one or two of these levels and find comfort in the knowledge that these are general landscapes that women find themselves exploring on the path to the actual relationship they desire.

I have also included a gift for you. For each person reading this book I am providing access to my Love Life Spectrum profiling tool. This is psychological profiling we have developed over many years to help you to discern the level of relating on the Spectrum from which you are currently operating. Once you discover this for yourself, you will make a giant leap forward in your ability to transform and grow into healthy relating patterns. To access this tool, click this link or type it into your browser:

https://belindabailey.com.au/the-love-codes-resources/

LOVE LIFE SPECTRUM LEVELS

Level 1 – Insulate

This level is marked by a stretch of aloneness and periods of loneliness. There is a very real sense of having no relationship prospects. Symptomatic of this stage is varying degrees of depression and despair. You may be hiding away from the world, either under your bed covers and avoiding social interactions and you're not taking care of your appearance nor making much of an effort to be your best self, in life in general.

This is the level of the spectrum that I was in when I first discovered my ex-husband's betrayal. I stayed home and avoided all contact with the outside world. I made up excuses to miss events and family gatherings and even started to avoid going to work. I took up smoking, and despaired at the thought of my future.

On the other end of the spectrum, you may be throwing

yourself into work, exercise, or other pursuits non-stop. Distractions like food, over-socializing and shopping—anything to avoid feeling your inner planes of emotions relating to your love-life circumstances—are in full swing. It's also possible that you are in a relationship and experiencing these symptoms of Insulate, in which case, it's probably time to address the underlying issues with some inner work, taking some time to recognize and transform the unconscious limiting beliefs around love and relationship.

The other characteristic of Level 1 is that in some way you are actually fearful of men. You suspect they have bad intentions or are untrustworthy or you're generally just angry with them on the whole. And so, you carry the mark of bitterness in terms of men and your relationship with them. This frame of mind overrides and sneaks up on you when you least expect it.

Level 2 – Frenetic Drive

This stage has urgency and panic. You are searching for a man and you're feeling frantic and desperate about it. This is different to Level 1 because you are aware that you desire a relationship but fear it will never happen. It is fear that drives you incessantly to try to manifest it.

When I was in Frenetic Drive, I felt as though I was fueled by my ovaries. You know that you're at this level because you're constantly thinking and talking about men. Whenever you're with your girlfriends, you find you're talking about men you know and don't know. You're discussing their private lives and trying to figure them out, what they want, what they're up to.

If you're in a relationship at this level, you'll find yourself trying to work out what you can do differently. There's a lot of over-thinking and even strategy coming in to play over your heart and feelings. You may also find you automatically take the blame for any problems in the relationship.

If single, you immediately see every man as a potential partner. As soon as a man walks into your reality, you size them up, envisage life with them and refer to The List. This stage can be a bit of a nightmare if left unchecked! Other aspects of your life start to suffer through neglect, your creativity becomes stifled and you lose touch with your sense of self because you are obsessing about men. It consumes all your energy, and other areas of your life begin to suffer.

At the level of Frenetic Drive, however, you may actually be starting to date men, but they are poor quality men that you wouldn't date if you were in your right mind. The red flag here is *you're* doing the pursuing. This does not necessarily mean you're the one calling and initiating dates, although it might. What it translates to is that you're constantly searching on date sites and social media for likely options. You're playing detective, looking up where he's going to be and what his interests are. You're deciphering the 'type' of woman he's into and if you happen to 'bump' into him on the dance floor, you're hanging around him intentionally! All of this behavior translates to pursuing, too.

Please note, symptomatic of Frenetic Drive is that the expression of your desires and feelings are disproportionate. You're a little on the crazy side of going crazy!

Level 3 – Frustrated to Hopeful

At Level 3, Frustrated to Hopeful, it begins to be a little more about the man than it does yourself. This is when you are likely to attract Mr Not Quite Right. He's so-so but not exactly right.

Symptomatic of this stage is that you are starting to wonder if there are any quality men left on planet Earth, and that there may be something inherently wrong with you. You're both doing the pursuing *and* being pursued. It's a mishmash of swinging in between. More often than not, you swing further towards the pursuing, just in case.

You're on this rollercoaster of hope and frustration. It's possibly my least favorite level and can be a real challenge to reign in. The rollercoaster extends itself to either one targeted man or with a string of men, one after the other. If one of them rings you and asks you out on a date then you immediately assume that he's extremely interested in you with an assumed longevity, so you're flying high and supremely confident. You feel like your first date is going very well, until he decides not to go home with you. You crash and burn and take an emotional dive into dark territory in a flash.

Whatever the circumstances, whether he calls back or not, you're on this relentless pendulum swinging between hope and frustration and back again. And when you do brush with intimate moments with men, you filter what you express so as to avoid pushing or scaring men away. This is not a pleasant or comfortable place to be, especially when you're stifling your true needs and feelings.

This is the level on the spectrum that my dear client and friend, Veronica, teetered on for many years. She even made a career out of it, hosting a popular internet show that was based on her misshapen dating escapades. It seemed funny when she spoke about it, and it kind of is when we look at it with hindsight. So much pendulum swinging but, in the end, it was the constant up and down and extreme highs and extreme lows of this level that drove her to seek me and the Love Codes out and change her experience.

Level 4 – Active Connecting

It's a big jump to this next level, Active Connecting, and once you get here, the view is serene. This is where you find yourself at a choice point for quality men and you genuinely believe in your dream relationship again. This is a wonderful place to be. You're not just hopeful but you believe 100% that it's going to manifest. The benefit of being at this level is that you are surrounded by a selection of good men. They are quality men with big hearts, good intentions, and purposeful lives.

If you happen to be in a relationship at this stage, you know deep down it's looking promising. No longer acting from a place of hopefulness, you are trusting the relationship unfolding at its natural pace and observe how the climate of the relationship is one of steady calm and good times. There may be an element of tension perhaps, considering long-term plans or commitments may not fully be cemented but this is exciting for you rather than causing doubt or anxiety.

You may recognize this level of the spectrum in your own life at some time, or it may remind you of my own story and when I started to turn 'would be lovers' into quality men stepping up to create a commitment. And it was not long after this that I met Warwick, the dream boat from Byron Bay.

At this level you might be turning down men who previously you would have given a chance, and other areas of your life are starting to pick up. You've got more energy, and this Active Connecting with the man of interest is actually *giving* you energy. There's a glow about you and you're confident expressing your authentic self. You're receiving validation for your creativity and self-expression from both your man and your other relationships too. I don't need to tell you, that this is an extremely healthy and fruitful place to be. It's a sign you've healed and evolved through many past hurts and relationships.

Level 5 – Evolutionary Relationship

This is the summit—the place that we want you to live and breathe in your ultimate relationship existence. You know when you're here because you're in a relationship where you feel calm and secure. It's a tenderly loving, soulful time to cherish with a beloved. You've got certainty. No doubts. You feel part of a team. You're making plans for the future together and he's proudly introducing you to the people in his life whenever he can. You're not only being truly loved but you are open to receiving love.

Your highest purpose is being fulfilled and you are on a path of your own mastery outside your intimate relationship. Sex is sensual love-making and transformative. You're still engaging in sneaky lunchtime rendezvous and playful dates if you want to but also entering sexual depths that are heart-opening and even spiritually awakening.

You feel safe to express your whole self, no longer filtering what you say or share, since you feel so at ease with your man and equally in love with yourself as you are with him. You feel at home in your own skin around him. Your natural self is shining. This is the kind of relationship you've been dreaming of.

♥

Since applying the Love Codes, I started to have great relationships. Until I was in my current marriage, I didn't know how good it could be. Evolutionary Relationship is in a league of its own. You can get here and stay here. This is the kind of relationship that heals, creates more love, and inspires both man and woman to rise to their greatest potential. It creates a sanctuary, a sacred haven to be cherished. This, my beautiful friends, this is where the Love Codes reside. This is where it all leads.

I highly recommend that you head to the link and answer the profiling questions so that you can discover which level you are at on the spectrum. Once you decipher this for yourself, the rest of this book will help you to make your way through the spectrum to reach Level 5 of Evolutionary Relationship.

Remember, too, these levels of relating are relevant to you if you are single or in a relationship and the change work that is connected to each level will have profound results in your life whether it be by attracting a higher quality relationship experience or transforming your current relationship into a healthier and more fulfilling one.

As you read on, you will come to see how other women just like you have moved from a Level 1, Insulate, all the way to Level 4 and eventually Level 5, Evolutionary Relationship.

Link to discover your Love Life Spectrum level:

https://belindabailey.com.au/the-love-codes-resources/

Chapter Highlights

- There is an unconscious primal need in men that only a woman can fulfil.

- We identified where you are on the love-life spectrum, realizing that each stage is all part of the process towards reaching a Level 5 Relationship.

- Whichever stage you are at, it is important to neither blame nor judge yourself. Each phase reveals to us more about ourselves and where there is room for growth.

- We also highlighted that the past can shape and block our future dreams if there has been heartache and the importance of healing in order to move on.

4

THE CODES

In this chapter we go in-depth with each of the Love Codes. I explain what they represent and how they play out in relating with men. I will be referring to real life examples to highlight how they operate, and demonstrate why it's so important to understand and embody each Code in order to cultivate a Level 5 relationship.

THE LOVE CODE FOUNDATION — THE QUANTUM RELATIONSHIP PARADIGM

This is the foundation of the Love Codes and the very basis of the entire map. Let's anchor it.

It is likely that you will never have come across this paradigm before and it is more than just a Code. It is the *purpose* of intimate relationships between a man and a woman, which is why it is the foundation of the Love Codes and very important.

The two aspects of relationship that women are generally caught up in are romance, where we get to soar to great heights and flights of peak states initiated by men in sensual, generous gestures; or the Business of Relationships, when we focus on buying a house, having a baby, building an empire and making concrete plans.

While these two aspects of a relationship are important, the deeper purpose behind relationships have too often been entirely overlooked and even suppressed by superficial desires. This is precisely what this principle will activate in you and your love life.

I invite you to consider the roles we play in modern relationships. In the past, there was a clear definition of the roles men and women were prepared for and conditioned to play. In your parents and grandparents' time, the man's role was to be the provider and the woman's role was to be the homemaker. It was cut and dry, until we continued to evolve into new phases of self-sovereignty, empowerment, and diversity.

Women, in particular, have claimed a lot more choice and control in their personal lives and the way we operate in the world; however, it hasn't quite clarified our roles in relationship and in many cases leads to confusion that can eventually become destructive.

Most commonly, when I ask women what they believe the current roles for men are in relationship, they tend to mention the provider/protector role, which is true to a degree. But what they fail to explore is an important dynamic within relationships that goes beyond the old paradigm. It is inspired by the archetype of The Hero. Your Hero.

And contrary to some popular belief, this isn't because men have bulging egos that need stroking, this is because men genuinely need to engage in challenges in order to grow. He basically does need to go hunting for monsters and dragons to be slayed in order to evolve—that's *how* he grows. We know this to be true through hormonal science and evidence-based research that indicates that as boys grow, they have varying levels of testosterone that literally propels them to take risks and overcome immediate danger and challenges.

This information has been very well explained and delivered by Steven Biddulph in his book *Raising Boys*.

You could say these are the building blocks of what makes a man; the challenges he has had to overcome in his life. As this is their natural way to transform and grow. So, too, in relationships do they seek opportunities for challenge. They are looking for opportunities to be The Hero.

It begins to get even more interesting when we look at the woman's role in a relationship. If I were to ask a woman what this role might be, she'll say what the next woman would say: EVERYTHING. And sadly, I have to agree. It has become the woman's role to be everything, despite this being impossible. You simply cannot be all things all the time, but we and society have placed expectation and pressure upon ourselves to do it all.

When our role was confined to the archetype of the homemaker, a role that many of us are not completely fond of, it revealed itself through the feminist movement to be a limited and narrow idea of a woman's capabilities, devastatingly oppressing her many gifts. Yet because this role has dominated our understanding of how a woman should feature in a relationship, and has become unacceptable to many, we are still discovering exactly what our role might be.

The fact that we never have been role modelled or taught the true wisdom of womanhood in relation to our primary, intimate partnerships, many of us are understandably disorientated when it comes to feeling secure in how we best figure in a man's life, in a way that is meaningful, empowered and even sacred. A role that expresses and honors all of who we are, all the time. This will undoubtedly resonate deeply with you on a soul level.

And it is this very thing that is at the heart of changing the paradigm of relationship once and for all. The truest and most holistic role for women in relationship is to be The Guide: the spiritual and emotional guide for her man.

The truest and most holistic role for women in relationship is to be The Guide: the spiritual and emotional guide for her man.

I know you have had at least one experience where you know what's best for your man, where it was as plain as day to you to know what or how would be the best way to go about something... but he won't for the life of him listen to you! Indeed, this is touching upon the truth of what it means to be his guide.

If you are able to truly receive and embody this deep and powerful kernel of wisdom, I assure you, it will dramatically alter how you relate with men and how they relate with you from now on.

Being the emotional and spiritual guide of the relationship is an honorable and beautiful role to uphold and I will walk you through how you can do this in a way that is in alignment with not only your heart's desires but with your connection to source energy; with the Divine. This will open your man to you, rather than push him away. You can unlock this natural and innate resource that is yet untapped and it is this that will catapult you directly towards a Level 5, Evolutionary Relationship on the Love Life Spectrum

Remember how I said that every man has an unconscious and primal need? This is exactly what that primal need is. For you to be the emotional and spiritual guide for him and the relationship. He wants you to. He needs you to. And the disappointing thing is that as women, we are so far from embodying this incredible state of being but when we do, we are a force to behold.

This brings us to the very important founding principle of the Love Codes Quantum Relationship Paradigm.

> *Woman is innately connected to the Divine and it is through her that man (and even mankind) will find his way back home.*

I invite you to truly meditate on this truth. Allow it to sink in and be integrated into what it means to you, to be a woman. When you apply this truth to your relationship with a man, when you fully trust and surrender to the divine life force moving through you. When you cultivate it, cherish it as sacred, find your own ways to honor it, and from that place, share it with the man you love, you are fulfilling your own purpose *and* assisting him to fulfil his purpose in life too. That, my friend, is the most attractive gift anyone can bestow upon another. To assist a man to fulfil his purpose in life, all the while honoring and cultivating your sacred connection with the Divine.

The truly beautiful thing is that this mystical quality to our relationships has no need to be verbalized. And yet, it is the thread that binds our love and devotion.

He needs you. They need us. And by cracking this part of the Love Codes you are on your way to blissful devotion built on a very grounded foundation of emotional and spiritual depth. That is true intimacy. That is authentic relating. That is the primitive dance of man and woman in passion and in love; building a truly modern and evolutionary relationship.

FEELINGS; THE TICKET
BACK TO LOVE

It's important to clarify exactly what it is when I mention the 'Divine.' While there are many ways to explain it, I am simply referring to something that is greater than yourself. It is beyond our small minds, untethered by definition from religious or spiritual dogma. And when you are living with the essence and influence of the Divine in your everyday life, you are in fact operating as a whole woman. For we are by nature, connected to the Divine, and the way we are innately connected to it is by a state called The Void.

The Void is a state of being that when in her prime state, comes effortlessly for a woman. It is the place from where creativity is born, where inspiration, imagination and feelings emerge. It isn't logical nor rational. It cannot be understood through the mind. This state, although also available to men, is much more readily available to women. We are weavers of our reality through communication with the subtle realms and energies of The Void, and as we tend to our own private relationship with it, we develop our own ways of communing.

It's interesting to note that the majority of spiritual and religious systems have been created by men and, for the most part, for men. Women have just had to 'fit in' with these concepts and for a long time did not have the opportunity to question nor challenge them.

In this new era of feminine leadership, the more we turn towards our inclination to be led by our intuition, our dreams, our sensuality and our instincts - all portals of The Void - the more we actually function from our natural essence as a woman. This is much more simple and pleasurable than adopting outdated systems that are not in tune with our nature.

This is not to say that women are more evolved or have a more enlightened perspective. This is just an honoring of our innate wisdom and ways. A wonderful illustration of this is the Kabbalist approach to life, the sacred text for the Mystic Jewish religion. It is an ancient system, respected by many, however women are not allowed to read it.

Contrary to popular belief, as explained by Karen Berg in *God Wears Lipstick*, when a woman is banned from a religious practice it is not because they think women are unworthy or of lesser intelligence. It is because within this ancient scripture it is understood that women have a direct connection to God and therefore do not need to study or read about it. They believed that if women did read the text, it would only confuse and muddy their already pure Divine connection.

Women *are* innately connected to the Divine through this void space which is accessed through the incredible interplay between our mind, body, and spirit. We have a direct channel, if you will, to higher states, enabling us to access beyond what the mind can comprehend and this doesn't occur through any sophisticated, learned, complex system. It is innate, activated and primarily expressed through our *feelings*.

That's right, our feelings. That which has been cursed many times over and often judged as wild, hysterical, or even madness. Our *feelings* when pure and unadulterated, bring us into direct communication with The Void, and when we can listen to and express our feelings in their integrity, then we step into the role as Guide for those around us, in particular our intimate partner.

It is important to impress here that feelings are not to be confused with emotions, which many women tend to stumble over from time to time. Part of what you will be learning through this book is how to tune in to your unadulterated feelings—as opposed to emotions—and express them constructively and with heart. Often you might think you're connected to your feelings, but I can guarantee that you are more likely being affected by or even over-ruled by your emotions.

We have been inundated with information telling us that being a person led by feelings isn't right; that it's not normal nor acceptable. That we need to tone it down and be practical, less sensitive and more logical and productive. We need to be efficient! And feelings just get in the way of efficiency.

Because of this overarching conditioning that has completely hijacked and dishonored our gift of feeling, we find ourselves doing one of two things, both of which are a hazard to relationships. The first of these two dysfunctional approaches is to suppress them and hide them away, compartmentalized and out of sight. The backlash to this approach means that they come out in perverted or unhealthy ways, which can eventually compel us to behave like monsters. Suppressing our feelings means they only gather energy and eventually find a crack to squeeze through, unleashed in disproportionate ways to the very thing we initially had feelings about.

The second dysfunctional approach we might take is avoidance through emotionalizing them. You see, a feeling is a simple state. When a feeling is free to be in its healthy and intended state, it is pure communication and moves through your body, expressing itself and then dissipates. But because our feeling nature has been misunderstood and demonized, when a feeling bubbles up we might try to rationalize it, analyze it, figure it out and introduce it to our mind, who then creates an emotion out of it. And even though this may seem like a natural progression and a reasonable way to process internally, it's not actually helpful in the long run. What it does, is to make 'sense' of something which is not supposed to be made sense of. It is supposed to be experienced.

Through the love codes you will come to understand that this is what we have been doing to our connection to something that is far greater than ourselves, which is where our power lies. We need to undo the demonization, so to speak, in order to achieve soulful, authentic and evolutionary relating with our partner.

We need to undo the emotional ties we've woven into the script of our feeling landscape and re-code our pathways of feeling so that when we are expressing ourselves, instead of alienating or pushing a man away, we are guiding them to a place of love and connection, just by being our beautiful self. Now wouldn't that be a wonderful place to be?

We need to replace the old programming that tells us that women and feelings are irrational and therefore bad—the narrative that women are supposed to be everything—and replace it with this quantum relationship paradigm programming.

Practice

Write down and repeat these two truths to yourself daily:

1. *A woman's role in a relationship is to be the guide – the spiritual and emotional guide for her man.*

2. *A woman is innately connected to the Divine and it is through her that man (and even mankind) will find his way back home.*

CODE 1 – ATTRACTIVE PERSUASION

Following on from this foundational principle is Code 1 – Attractive Persuasion. This Code enables us to understand the importance and function of 'attracting' men and not just having them around. If you are committed to this journey of improving your love life to align with your dreams, then it requires you to be ready to set aside everything that you think you have known so that you can be left open and willing to learn something entirely new. Remember when I spoke about the moment I realized that if I wanted the dream then I needed to be vulnerable, I needed to be willing to be wounded, to open my heart wide. This is your moment of truth. Are you ready to be truly vulnerable and open your heart wide to something that may feel contrary at first?

When discovering the common pattern in women that have successful relationships, this is the key area I found that runs deep and broad across intimate relating. It is of great importance that men are actively pursuing you, and this remains true whether you are dating or in a committed relationship already.

This is not because of the classic assumption that men need to be in control, and we must submit. This is more to do with the law of attraction and the quantum world. And so, the natural question and frustration for women becomes, how do you make this happen when you have no control over the actions of a man? You can't *make* a man pursue you.

While this was one of the things that frustrated the hell out of me during my dating life, I soon learned that it had nothing to with what I said, how I looked or what air of mystery

I was putting out into their attention field. It has instead, everything to do with the "law of polarity." Just as we have polarity in magnets with positive and negative poles attracted to each other, we know that all energy can have a negative and positive charge. This applies to our knowledge of masculine and feminine energy.

These terms are not gender specific—we all possess both masculine and feminine energy—and in the case of man and woman in a relationship, I will be applying the masculine energy to the man and the feminine to the woman, to illustrate how these opposites attract. Men are generally more at home in, and more often in their masculine polarity and women are generally more at home in their feminine polarity. However, women have been derailed over the years to extend themselves to occupy the masculine domain in order to gain equal footing with men in many arenas.

In the Western world, as a general statement, women have become more masculinized *and* we live in a masculine dominated world. It is a world of 'doing' rather than 'being.' Of getting out there and making things happen and if you can't keep up, you'll be left behind. As a result, both men and women are operating in masculine modes of behavior which diminishes the forces of attraction. This is big news, because it means that if you are operating more dominantly from your masculine polarity, which almost all women are, then this is negatively affecting your potential relationships AND it is not exactly your fault. It is more rightly an effect of the cultural conditioning that has caused a generation of unbalanced societal views and expectations and therefore unconscious destructive beliefs around love and relationship.

Switching into a more feminine essence does not necessarily mean prioritizing your prettiness and polishing your nails, even though that can be enjoyable. For a man to have a natural attraction to you he needs to feel safe around you, and it does not feel safe for a man to be around a pronounced masculine energy within you.

> *"It does not feel safe for a man to be around a pronounced masculine energy within you."*

As we have discussed, men are geared for protection and alertness to potential competition or danger. To illustrate this, we just need to take notice when a man walks into a room among other men, even if they are all friends. They check each other out, puff up their chest and present the firmest handshake they can. This primitive behavior dates to a time when we would need the strongest men in the tribe to pick up their weapons and protect us. Even though this dynamic has shifted over time it is still part of a man's nature and psychology to serve through protection.

I invite you to observe a man in his masculine energy taking off into the world and you'll notice it is akin to a warrior setting foot on a battlefield. The image of picking up a big stick and heading out into the world depicts the classic masculine way in motion.

Women can also do this now. We have the right, that we have fought for, to pick up our sticks in the world and represent what we are passionate about. We make our own mark. Claim our own territory and isn't this a wonderful change, something that our ancestors fought for through feminist revolution.

Whilst this new-found ability to embody our own masculine has its gifts and is our birth-right to be able to access our own masculine energy when we want to and when it is helpful, it is our inability to move dexterously between the two polarities, remaining stuck in the masculine that has, inadvertently, tarnished the world of relating between men and women and is potentially ruining relationships. What's become apparent is that women, in all innocence and pursuit of following their drive and purpose, forget to put the stick down. It is something we all need to grow aware of if we are going to be habitually stepping into our masculine in pursuit of our dreams, alongside creating an intimate and passionate affair based on real attraction.

If this has become second nature to you, then now is the time to practice putting your stick down with the intention of gracefully entering the gentle force-field of the feminine. What we need to re-learn to do, is that once we have put down our sticks, we need to pick up our ability to exist within our innate feminine framework—the creative, collaborative, patient, compassionate, receptive self.

I call this Fairyland and I use this term for several reasons, one of them is because it pushes my buttons with connotations of being weak and silly which is precisely the problem with judgement of all things non-rational! I know it triggers a lot of strong-willed women in this way, which therefore gives it power. It also conjures feelings and images of being immersed in the imaginary landscape of fertile breeding ground for our feminine self to blossom.

Here we have two equally important polar-opposite worlds

of battle sticks and Fairyland that illustrate the interplay of the masculine and the feminine. If we look to others in the world who have not yet been corrupted by social expectations, you will notice how young boys gravitate towards sticks and stones and bashing and crashing, and young girls will fuss and frolic in their Fairyland, imagining little castles and winged-beings into reality. While there are crossovers to these gender roles and all children have the capacity to explore all styles of play, there are undeniable trends and stereotypes that unfold into our more mature ways of relating into adulthood.

Momentarily take yourself back to the image of young children immersed in their imaginative world of play. The boys are being rambunctious rascals and the girls are fluttering through imaginative landscapes. If a little girl wanted to snatch the attention of a boy and she pulled them over to look at her fairies, the little boy would most likely bash the fairy on its head, right?

On the other hand, if the little girl remained happily absorbed in her wonderland and the boy looks over, and she does nothing, what do you think might happen? He becomes intrigued. He wanders over to see what it's all about. He may still tug at her hair or poke her with a stick to get her attention; however, as he grows into a man he hopefully takes the approach of a gentlemen to engage her attention. I see this all the time with my son and his female friends; it still surprises me just how true it is.

The point here is, when you are in your Fairyland, I guarantee that men are completely intrigued and magnetically attracted to you. They are drawn towards you. But as soon as you pick up your stick, they ready themselves for battle because that's how men interact with the masculine polarity. You can even decipher it in the vocabulary they use when they speak to each other. In a conversation between men they might say: 'We won that one,' or, 'I can't win with her,' or 'Gee man, it's a real battlefield out there.' They are referring to our nature when we are in the masculine polarity, when we haven't put our sticks down and they meet you as an opponent.

When you're gripping your sticks, they are not *attracted* to you, not in the way you want them to be and you risk ending up in the friend-zone. He says things like, 'I love hanging out with her, she's cool,' but he's not undeniably attracted to you, not in the way that starts real and lasting relationships. He might be attracted to you for some sexual expression because masculine energy can be fun and explosive sexually. But it almost never translates into long-term lasting attraction and committed relationship where the attraction and polarity lasts.

As soon as you step into Fairyland, it's like a light switches on. I remember in my own journey when I made the switch consciously. Some of my long-term male friends began to tell me that they started to develop feelings for me! It was a very eye-opening, rapid movement.

The important key to note here is that your men are actually starting to feel safe around you. That's the allure and the pull. You may not have previously appreciated that it is quite scary for a man to approach women with their sticks up, if they want to explore intimacy with you. So, embrace the practice of putting down your stick and instead, slipping on your fairy wings. With sound knowledge that this does not at any time and in any way mean being disempowered. Quite the opposite in fact as you will see more deeply as we continue our journey.

LOVE CHRONICLE #4

Whenever I discuss Attractive Persuasion, I love to tell a story about a beautiful client of mine, Marietta, a forty-two-year-old vivacious woman who runs her own successful health clinic and enjoys the abundance of travel with friends and socializing in high-end places. She has achieved everything she's wanted in her adult life except a loving, committed relationship. When Marietta called me, she'd been single and more-often-than-not dateless for eight years.

This is a highly intelligent, attractive, radiant, and fun-loving woman; someone you could easily and would want to make friends with. But despite all these wonderful qualities she still wasn't attracting men or being pursued by them. So, she jumped into the extended Love Codes training to turn her love life around. We were only one module into the program when she experienced her first dramatic shift.

It occurred one evening when she attended a dinner event with friends. She was sitting around the table and sharing about her studies with me and the Love Codes and specifically divulged the magic of Attractive Persuasion. One of her friends grew annoyed and even irritated by her sharing, saying that it sounded like a load of rubbish and why should we be the one to make changes. Very often when we have integrated this new knowledge into our lives, a sure sign it is taking affect can be highlighted by these instances in friendships where someone gets triggered and rubs up against your newfound growth point. It seems to activate within them a fear that they are losing you to an unknown and new way and it can make them feel uncomfortable. It's a good sign, and on this particular evening, Marietta, in her own graceful style let it roll off her back and continued enjoying her night.

As the dinner progressed, Marietta had more than one man approach her to engage in conversation with genuine interest. One man even expressed that he found her intriguing and just had to talk to her, despite admitting he felt a little awkward being so forward. As their conversation progressed, another man began hovering near her for a while, who eventually just butted into their discussion to get her attention. The first guy wasn't budging any time soon and Marietta found it quite comical watching these two men unconsciously competing for her attention. She also felt a rush of gratitude for evoking this behavior from what appeared to be quality men after such a dearth of opportunity and attention.

Fast forward to the latter part of the evening, and a completely different man asked her to dance, to which she accepted. While enjoying the dancefloor she quickly noticed that the two previous men had made their way close by her, trying to get her attention with suave movements and a little eye-contact. She found it fun and hilarious and had such a playful and spirited time in all the men's presence. But what Marietta found most memorable, was when her friend who had previously criticized her for the positive changes she was making in her love life, approached her to apologize, for she could see that whatever Marietta was doing, was working!

And this is why I do what I do, to receive the late-night texts from Marietta brimming with overwhelming delight having unlocked her innate power of attraction, as well as the

> *wisdom, to embrace all facets of her love life in a way that is*
> *empowering and natural. I get emotional just recalling how*
> *the Love Codes take effect in real time and cherish the healing*
> *that comes when we start experiencing these precious and*
> *exciting moments with men.*

I invite you to take notice of what happens in your dynamic with men when you remember to put your Fairyland wings on ready to soar. At first, this may seem unnatural or a tad vulnerable or may even feel like a hard habit to crack because it is different to having your stick up if you have grown used to exerting directive energy in the world. I can assure you though, it will begin to be pleasurable and a relief to return home to your feminine self, and it will have a ripple effect creating radical shifts in your personal affairs with men.

Now once you've got yourself attracting quality men, you need to start considering what the heck you're going to do with them!

CODE 2 – INVISIBLE INFLUENCE

Invisible Influence delivers you the pleasure of finding yourself in the company of men who want to give you what you truly desire. This is because once we are attracting men to us by way of Code 1 (Attractive Persuasion) you could find yourself surrounded by all manner of men. Whilst this may be a welcome change to a near drought, it is then important to qualify the type of men you are engaging with. One of the gravest mistakes many of us have made in the past is judging a man on outdated filters that are based on our old limiting beliefs. More often than not, we end up looking past the really great men who have needed a simple activating ingredient from us to step up into being the man that we really want them to be. This is where Code 2, Invisible Influence is essential.

This Code is about inspiring a man to step up to offer you the love, respect, passion, and commitment that you are yearning for.

Even more than that, Code 2 unlocks your ability to greatly influence a man's potential. Now this is a controversial subject as we've all been told before never to date a man for his potential, that it leads to false promises and delusions. But this is where I disagree. I would tweak this advice to say: Never date a man for his potential *unless* you have this Invisible Influence. This is because you are beginning to understand that a man is greatly influenced in his purpose and direction by a woman who is embodying her full power and innate wisdom. One could say, an awakened woman is the activating ingredient for a man's potential.

> *One could say, an awakened woman is the activating ingredient for a man's potential.*

Remember how *Every man has an unconscious and primal need to be the Hero, to make his woman happy?* Well, you see, there are a lot of men who need to and want to, step up and be The Hero; to be exceptional at offering their gifts to the world and be in a committed and loving relationship. But he's going to keep playing around like a teenager until he has been exposed to that activating ingredient.

You know the saying, behind every great man is a great woman? This is where it originated. From that alchemical process that ignites when a man encounters a woman who sparks his potential simply by being her beautiful self. When you have mastered the Code of Invisible Influence, you will quite literally see men change from being mediocre men into incredible men—the kind of breath-taking, quietly confident, realized masculinity that women find both attractive and on par with their deepest dreams.

This is the perfect place to mention that this has nothing to do with telling a man what to do. In fact, it is almost the opposite to that approach. If you tell him what to do, that he should 'go for that promotion,' or 'change his diet,' or do something differently than he has set out to do, you will get one of two outcomes, both of which lead to a deterioration of your magnetic attraction.

He will either:

1. Do it, and by doing so, time and time again, he will end up feeling emasculated and stripped of his role as The Hero. He will slowly unravel and surrender more into his feminine self. When this happens, we usually lose our attraction and desire for him or we find ourselves become more masculine. I often see this dynamic playing out in couples where the woman is so frustrated with her man not behaving like The Man; that she feels forced to play the more active role in the relationship. Little does the woman realize that this dynamic has been seeded by her own behavior of *telling* him what to do.

2. Say no, and often he will say no to save his own sense of masculinity. When a man says no in this way, the attraction levels are maintained because the polarity is maintained; however, the relationship itself is unhealthy and we begin to feel as though he isn't caring about us and he begins to feel like he can't 'win' with you. Meaning if he can't be the hero and fulfil his innate role, eventually he will lose interest. These, unfortunately, are the situations; however, where we can't help but go back for more of the same undesirable treatment. This is partly due to the fact he has remained in his masculine energy which retains the attraction but his reluctance to give you what you want has driven a wedge between you.

In addition to these negative outcomes, this behavior also does not give you the desired outcome of having him compelled to step up into the best version of himself. We know that the notion of not telling a man what to do is not entirely new. However, never sharing with him what you want or want him to do can lead to an extremely unexpressed, dissatisfied woman. Match this to our foundational truth that it is our role to emotionally and spiritually guide the relationship, it becomes obvious that we need to prime ourselves with Invisible Influence behaviors to keep that magnetic dynamic alive. This allows him to choose for himself that which aligns with your deepest desires whilst he remains sovereign in making that choice for himself.

I would love now to share with you a very simple and effective formula that I teach all the graduates of the Love Codes which makes it really simple and easy to break it down and understand exactly HOW to incorporate this Invisible Influence in a way that remains integral and authentic to your unique self.

This one pathway is a way to use your communication as a means to engage this Code. If you follow the sequence below then you will find that you are beginning to embody this Code and start to reap the benefits.

The thing to remain mindful of with this formula is that ultimately men need to be the hero. They feel like they are being the hero when they see you are 'happy.' They will internally take responsibility for your state, whether they are aware of it or not. This means that if you are always dissatisfied or disgruntled, they will be feeling, often unconsciously, that it is their fault. They may not admit this to you or to anyone else, but more often than not, deep down lies a long-held fear that they are not good enough or even just plainly not good. This holds true also for the instances when you are happy or satisfied. Likewise, they will often internally take responsibility for this as well, whether it is their responsibility or not. Which means that they feel like they are winning when you are happy and satisfied. It's really a good outcome for all.

So, when there is something that you would like from him, something as simple as for him to remember to turn the light on for you when you are going to be home late, to something more emotionally helpful, like to simply hold you when you are feeling overwhelmed. When we ask for it, or share this desire using this simple and authentic formula, you will find that he willingly offers you the behavior because it provides both of you with your desired outcome. For you, the thing you deeply desire. And for him, being your hero.

INVISIBLE INFLUENCE FORMULA

Express and communicate to your man the following:

1. What you want

2. What you feel

3. His prize

Let me illustrate how this works for you a little more deeply. When we can express to our man how something makes us feel and what it gifts him with, he will willingly do all he can to provide us with that thing.

This formula makes me recall a Love Codes graduate who had spent years trying to get her husband to leave the light on for her when she worked late. He would do it once and then forget again and again. It drove her nuts! And this went on literally for years. Until she applied this formula. She waited for the next time that he DID leave the light on and then she said to him:

'Darling, when you left the light on for me last night' (=Number 1 in the formula—*What I want*)

'I felt so safe and cared for' (= Number 2 in the formula—*What I feel*).

'It makes me feel so relaxed and like I want to connect with you' (= Number 3 in formula—*His prize*).

In their situation, he knew that connect meant he had the opportunity for intimacy.

Do I need to say that ever since that night, he ALWAYS leaves the light on when she works late now? This may seem a trivial thing to some of us, but just imagine where else this could be applied!

I should relay here, that often, number 2 IS number 3. Saying how it makes me feel 'happy,' 'relaxed,' 'open' is often enough of a 'prize' for your man, because remember his goal is to make you happy. But for extra kick and points we go for also sharing something that is specific to him.

Now at first glance, this may seem a little flowery or over the top. But I promise you that once you try it on, it feels very natural and right. This is because this way of communicating is a lot more natural for women, although we have been indoctrinated into the masculine, overly directive way of speaking and so it takes a bit of practice to come back to our 'native' tongue.

Recap for the Invisible Influence Formula:

1. Decide what you want.

2. Express exactly what it is that your 'want' will provide you with as far as a 'feeling' goes. (Remember here that for your man, part of being The Hero is also being The Provider.)

3. Determine what his prize is when you feel this way and share that too. Hint: It will always be a form of making you happy and may be the same as number 2.

4. It is also helpful to observe and then acknowledge him for when he does it, by showing how it makes you happy. Therefore, he wins and so do you!

What I find striking here is the sadness I witness among women when they gain this knowledge then realize that in hindsight, it could have benefited or even saved a previous relationship that became stifled in an unhealthy dynamic. I think it is important to acknowledge how past relationships may have turned out very differently had we acquired such wisdom then, or that many men could have actually become incredible men if you had known this much overlooked, hidden dynamic was always available to you. But we need to look upon our past love life with a balanced perspective of gratitude for the lessons gained and take this new wisdom into our future (or current) romance.

To remember Invisible Influence and how important it is, I want to share with you a relationship mantra that can be recited silently to yourself, even in the company of your man. But first I want to remind you of your sacred role in the relationship—*to be the guide*—in that you are controlling the direction of the relationship. This is a very enlivening thing for many women to learn. That it is our role to 'control' by way of guidance, the outcome of the relationship! It is his role to be The Hero and The Champion. He needs to feel like he is winning because to him, life is a metaphor for some sort of competition. And the incredible thing is that when you are comfortable in your role as The Guide and allow him to be The Hero, then you get to steer the direction of the relationship and he gets to be the winner. Notice how the interplay is akin to a harmonious, synergetic tango?

Here is the mantra:

I am in control by having my man win .

I am in control by having my man win .

I am in control by having my man win .

One of the most valuable reasons to have Invisible Influence is deciding that it is more important for you to *have what you want* than it is to be right or even the winner.

Now that we understand the importance of putting down our battle sticks, this also emphasizes releasing the need to win too. When we drop our sticks and slip on our fairy wings, we are honoring our true needs by valuing the importance of us getting what we want, and that in order to get what we want we need to let go of the need to be the winner. This is Invisible Influence working its undercover magical effect.

So remember:

I am in control by having my man win.

Now the phrase, *I am in control*, is known to ruffle feathers. Have you ever been told by a man that you are a control freak? He may well have been right! Although, it is a judgmental statement that has been projected through the cultural misappropriation of feminine qualities. In actual fact, it is your true and healthy role to be in control of the direction of the relationship to some degree, we've just not been role modelled how to do this in a healthy way. Hence, it has become expressed and misunderstood in perverted ways.

The other topic worth raising is that there is this assumption that we shouldn't let a man win because it means we are losing, or submitting, yet I believe this could not be further from the truth. What you need to understand here is that the thing he ultimately wants to win, is you! He desires being your hero, so inevitably, allowing him to win with you, will be getting you what you want too. It is win/win, and it makes a lot more sense that men and women were created to fulfil and love each other in this way, than the popular belief that we are so different that we repel each other. This simply isn't true. We are wired to communicate and intimately express our true selves, with grace.

So when you know what you want and you present this to your man, you are, in a way, presenting him with a manual or cheat sheet on how to win with you because all he wants to do is feel like he is The Hero. Your Hero. Remember, he doesn't want you to tell him how to do it because this leaves him no choice but to be emasculated or say no and drive a wedge through the relationship. These outcomes, as we discovered earlier, aren't ideal for either party involved.

You can see how you are in control but in a healthy, balanced way. You can and will receive all that you want from a man and your relationship with him, and not solely when you are in the dating phase, as this extends to the longevity of your chosen partnership. Even with the men around you, if you understand that you're in control by letting him win, this will create a positive engagement between you both and the male population in general.

LOVE CHRONICLE #5

I recall having an intimate dinner party where I invited a few of my male friends as well as my girlfriends. It was during a time in my life that I was quite the gypsy, often moving around because I liked to change my environment and not settle anywhere for too long. On this occasion I was warming my new home with dinner and with friends, when I overheard a conversation held by some of the men.

They were telling each other how they had helped me move house, as I'd asked a few of them favors along the way. And they were comparing and competing about who had done the most for me! It was quite adorable, and I had a little chuckle to myself, knowing that the Code of Invisible Influence had inspired their action and their pride in performing it.

They all wanted to be the one who had done the most for me, to be The Hero, not because I was a particularly special woman whom they were pursuing but simply because they were gifted the opportunity to be my hero during the arduous task of moving house. What I have learned from the artful application of this Code is that it's so innate, for both man and woman, and I love witnessing how we all get to feel good, in our special masculine or feminine way, about the intended outcomes.

I have outlined above the formula for Invisible Influence that details in clear steps how to communicate with your man in a way that gets what you want, and allows him to be The Hero. Enjoy this practice while watching the favorable results unfold for both of you.

CODE 3 – HEARTBREAK NO MORE

Wouldn't it be wonderful to feel secure in the knowledge that we never have to return to that dismal place of devastating heartbreak? Crack this Code and you're there. Just like Dorothy in the *Wizard of Oz*, you are well and truly on the journey now if you can stick to the Yellow Brick Road that inevitably leads to your dream destination. You may need to overcome obstacles along the way but if you keep returning to the path set before you and keep your eye on the prize of the ideal relationship you are manifesting, then it is possible. Just like Dorothy, when you arrive at your dream destination in the arms of your man you will live and breathe in the space of Heartbreak No More.

At this point you have men expressing their love and respect for you by doing what you want and you, in turn, are activating them to reach their potential. There may be a selection of quality men around you to choose from and because great men are now compelled towards you, you want to ensure you're making the best choice. You want to be with a man who is in line with all that you desire from an intimate, primary relationship. I want you to imagine it like this:

You're on a path that happens to be a Yellow Brick Road. At the end of the path is your goal—this is your ideal, dream relationship. Just like the dreams I previously asked you to imagine before, that 'level' of relationship is right at the top end of your Yellow Brick Road, so you want to keep walking towards it. Alternatively, and all too often, what actually happens is that when we are on our path going towards our goal, at some point a man comes along who we think is above the average mark so we decide to date him. We may even end up in a relationship with him, however, it occasionally turns out that he might not be quite in line with our end goal. He's on another path.

Rather than keeping on with your own path to your cherished destination, you veer off track to be with him. When this happens it's an indication that we're not as committed to our goal as we thought and instead, invest time and energy with him and developing the relationship. We venture far off track in a direction more so dictated by him and eventually realize that it's not what we really want, or he decides to leave having realized himself that you're on different paths. This is what happens when we start to focus on the man rather than the goal.

We suddenly find ourselves alone and in unfamiliar territory, so far off track perhaps having lost time and traction, needing to make our way back to our beloved Yellow Brick Road where we left off, six weeks, six months, six years later! Sadly, we usually have to make our way back to the beginning because, due to this minor diversion, we have lost trust in ourselves, in the process and perhaps in men too. We may even have given parts of our self away. We inadvertently create more work for ourselves in having to remove more blocks in the way of us getting to our dreams, if only we had stuck to our path!

The reason this happens (and it happens to all of us) is because of those deeply ingrained, destructive beliefs we have around relationships. If you recall the blurt exercise that is designed to expose these distortions and false ideas, then you'll understand the power they can hold over our true desires. We learned that the unconscious mind is not programmed for your dreams, so when you veer off the Yellow Brick Road to be with this Not Quite Right Man, you are following unconscious belief systems. You are following situations that confirm those blurts to be true—that you're not good enough, men are all the same, you're too much for them and they don't want to commit. Whatever it is that you truly believe has the potential to steer you off your path, so be aware.

To counteract this distraction, you need to be committed to your end goal, that Level 5 Relationship reflective of your ideal, dream commitment with a man in love. Your dedication here will make all the difference by way of supporting yourself through the journey of finding true love. Some days it might require grit. Other days you will feel more relaxed by your inner knowing that it's where you're heading.

When you hold true to your vision and you meet a man who you like and he likes you, you begin to walk side-by-side on the journey to your destination. If and when you get to the point where he simply does not align with your direction, he simply veers off in a different way and you continue heading towards your goal, unscathed and staying true to your heart.

Later down the track, you will meet another man. The wonderful thing about having maintained commitment to your Yellow Brick Road means that each man you stumble across indicates that you are closer and closer to your dream. You have gained so much wisdom and experience along the way and are attracting your match with clarity and trust. Every man you meet will be closer in frequency match to the ultimate goal. Wherever you leave off with the last one, will be where you start off with the next.

I want to drive this next aspect home. If there's no man around, you do not have to stop the relationship momentum. In fact, you continue the flow by putting in the work, tending to your Fairyland, cultivating your feminine essence and remaining open to receiving your dreams. Men will come to meet you. They will be drawn to you, and one of the most valuable side-effects of Heartbreak No More is that the potential for heartbreak dissolves. Where it might have taken you years to recover from heartbreak before, you are now setting your self up on the adventure of love to remain true to your vision, and that's that. Men will come and go and your radar will keep you on track whether they are in alignment or not.

Of course, you will journey through the natural ebb and flow of loving and letting go of the men you meet who are Not Quite Right and this is an essential part of your humanity. You might have a cry, a natural grieving process proportionate to the loss. You go out with your girlfriends, have a night of chick-flicks and wine, perhaps even a one-night-stand or steamy fling! But you keep going. You get back on track and it's a very different and much more positive, love-life adventure, because you are always aligned and inspired by your end goal.

Although it can be disturbing to know that those darn blurts are impacting, influencing and even creating what you attract. It is also enlightening and relieving to learn because it starts to make sense as to why it is that we are often attracted to men that end in disappointment.

Have you ever wondered why you are just not 'into' the men that are really interested in you? Someone who looks and sounds like everything you've ever wanted, who treats you like royalty and gives you the world *but* you are just not that into him. Or, on the other hand, the one you find the most appealing is the one who doesn't want to commit, he hasn't got his own life together, he's a bit of a mess on all fronts, is insensitive to your needs and not even into you, yet *he* is the one you find most appealing?! You're not alone. I come across this conundrum with women all the time and it is a deeply disruptive element to attraction that stems from the foundations of how attraction actually works.

Attraction, in very simple terms, forms in two ways:

1. Biological attraction, whereby your DNA recognizes his DNA as a good match to create children.

2. Attraction through unconscious belief systems, where you are looking for a match to prove underlying beliefs correct. (Remember, you are drawn to situations that will give you an experience that confirms your beliefs to be right.)

If your unconscious beliefs about your ideal relationship are 'I'm not good enough' or 'It's too late,' then you will unconsciously be drawn to and attracted to situations that will siren, 'Yes, you're right!'

And so you meet a man, and he seems incredible and you are deeply attracted to him and he may even, on the surface, be entirely different to all the other men you've previously dated. Be mindful that you will be drawn to something in him that will end up providing you with an experience to match your Poison Blurt. Your attraction *may* have steered you off track, off the Yellow Brick Road. And you may wonder, what's the solution to overcoming these sneaky blurts and their power? Only date men that I'm not really attracted to?!

No! What is required is to re-code our unconscious mind to match our ultimate goal. We need to eliminate all the Poison Blurts that are sabotaging your dreams. We need to reprogram and rewrite those blurts so that you are now attracted and drawn to your dream man and the type of relationship you want to share with him. Once you have achieved this, you will find yourself attracted to men that are very good for you, who will be walking you closer to your goal rather than down the garden path.

Have you ever been attracted to the wrong guy? Well, I certainly have, more than once! And I still joke around about how my now husband is not the kind of guy I would ever have dated in the past. His job, his friends, his looks, I would never have previously found appealing and so in my mind when I met him, I thought, 'This is a bit weird!' I was definitely attracted to him and following my Yellow Brick Road and reading all the signs and signals along the way pointing me towards him too, yet if I had met him five years earlier, I'm not so sure we would have ever been together.

Now, we are married. My girlfriends describe him as *not normal* because he is incredibly loving, romantic, successful, handsome and respects me—all the things a woman dreams about! Had I not erased those pesky blurts lurking in the recesses of my mind I would have missed out on this dream being realized, which makes me wonder how many people are missing out along the way due to the unchecked rulings of their unconscious mind. Don't let this be you. Do the Poison Blurt exercise, more than once.

Remain committed, even fanatically devoted, to your end goal coming to fruition. And re-code those blurts!

CODE 4 – THE VULNERABILITY LOOP

The fourth Code, The Vulnerability Loop, is extremely important to master. By now you have chosen your own version of Mr. Right or are choosing good men to share yourself with intimately.

You've attracted good quality men and you've inspired them to step up and offer you what you want. Congratulations! You've traversed some huge growth curves and evolved beyond a lot of redundant relationship behaviors. Now it's time to deepen your connection with the man you are feeling most aligned with, to be able to take the relationship to the next level.

Vulnerability is a hot topic, possibly done to death in many personal development circles, which demonstrates that it is of real value to people and that being vulnerable is something we all need some relearning to be able to do. To be able to show your vulnerability is a step in the direction of falling in love. In fact, I would go so far as to say it is *how* we fall in love. When I speak of falling in love, I'm not referring to fairy-tale spin offs, I'm talking about the kind of love you feel with someone as though you have arrived home or are in the embrace of soul family.

It is a texture of love whereby you finally feel as though you know who you are. You see all of yourself in its entirety because someone is meeting all parts of you with unconditional love; parts you may never have seen in yourself. It is a profound experience that I wish for every woman to experience in their lifetime and I trust that these Codes will support your endeavor to find it for yourself.

To fall in love, we need vulnerability. And yet there are two distinct destructive patterns that are commonly engaged when it comes to vulnerability and relating.

When we first arrive in this world, we are clearly vulnerable; however, as we grow older we are hurt and challenged by life circumstances. You may have been betrayed or, as with myself, encountered abusive, toxic relationships that required much healing. These become very real reasons to not be vulnerable or even to lose touch with our own vulnerability. We close it down as an act of protection and while this has some validity, it does not assist our personal relationships to grow and strengthen in their depth of love and connection.

The other hurdle relative to vulnerability is the opposite to this pattern, where you know that it is important to be vulnerable so you want to show your vulnerability and trust in the connection you're forming with a man, so you rapidly expose everything about yourself. What you're feeling and what's stirring within is very quickly drowned in the avalanche of rapid opening up. And I don't judge anyone for this either. With all the competing information out there telling us that we must be vulnerable to be able to be loved, is it any wonder that we stumble through in an over-sharing mode, to discover it can be just as damaging as not being vulnerable at all.

If we choose to withhold our vulnerability then we will never connect deeply with a man, yet in order to share our vulnerability in a mature and healthy way, we also need to build trust and healthy boundaries—another two trending concepts that get discussed often but with a lack of real guidance as to how to create and foster them within an intimate relationship.

If you've found yourself in the over-sharing group of vulnerability then you may have noticed that this is generally overwhelming for the receiver, who might then retreat or completely run in the opposite direction. So again, the wisdom lies in knowing how to build trust and at the same time, create healthy boundaries that will be the container for your vulnerability to be expressed safely, freely, and in its own beautiful way.

When we are young it comes more naturally to be vulnerable. Our innate vulnerability extends itself to all kinds of situations because we've had less experiences that may have tarnished or threatened us. As we mature and encounter more relationships and therefore more opportunities and risks for getting hurt, we may have endured enough to suggest that it's not safe to be vulnerable and we start to build stone walls around our tender heart.

I'm here to assure you that you can be vulnerable whilst trusting in the wisdom you have gained from past experiences without the naivety of a child running the show, who throws caution to the wind in dangerous situations. With the Vulnerability Loop activated and embodied when relating with men, you will begin to trust the process of falling in love through the exquisite, heart-melting balm of shared vulnerability. It will guide you to be vulnerable and have trust in situations that are safe and invite openness, and it will help you to avoid being heartbroken to the point of complete devastation. Many of us completely shut down to avoid heartbreak all together, which raises a huge block between you and where you want to be: in love. Not with the Vulnerability Loop in full-circular motion.

Vulnerability and trust go hand-in-hand. While men need us to be vulnerable in order for them to fall in love with us, women need to be able to trust a man in order to be able to fall in love with him. And so, this dance of vulnerability and trust sets the tone of a rich and fulfilling relationship, shaped by loving boundaries and clear communication.

To illustrate the Vulnerability Loop, I want you to imagine yourself surrounded by layers of circles, like onion rings forming crystalline over your entire being. In the middle of your core there is another small circle. At this center point—the core of who you are stripped bare—is where you hold all your dreams and fears, your shadows and hidden aspects, the parts of yourself you don't quite accept and those you also treasure. It is the doorway to The Void—your feelings and creativity. It is the place where men yearn to meet you at your very center.

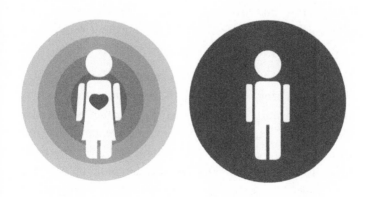

Each of the circles surrounding you is a layer of protection, guarding you from potential hurt. The most outer layer is what you present to the world on the surface while the very center is shared with but a few trusted confidants. Sadly, for many people, this sacred space is often not shared with anyone.

When this core of you is exposed, it is when you might feel most unsafe because you can't always predict how it will express itself and whether it will be accepted. So you feel a strong need to protect it. To remain fully guarded all the time however, sabotages your experience of falling in love. Men want to see you through the lens of vulnerability. They want to look past those surface layers and connect with you at the core of your being. Their love for you can translate into acceptance of all that you are, but you have to let them in.

When you first meet someone you arrive with all these layers around you like skins. If you were to quickly undress, you risk frightening them off with too much too soon! Remember, it has taken you a whole lifetime to come to know these parts of yourself, it takes time to absorb so much. Consider it a seductive, alluring undressing of the exquisite jewel that you are. Approach each layer with the touch of grace and self-care.

An avalanche of feelings and shadows alongside the sheer velocity of sharing your dreams and expectations with a man from the outset, is a tad overboard for a man who is also integrating the activation of his own sensitive nature by your sheer radiance. So go slowly. One step, one layer at a time. This is also how we keep ourselves safe and build up trust in a relationship. It's also how we determine whether the man we are exploring these deeper aspects with has the ability to hold and cherish us.

The other common way people use or misuse vulnerability is that rather than presenting with flexible, organic layers reflective of their true nature, they create walls of steel. These tend to have the effect of projecting onto a man that he has to prove that you can trust him, and until then, you won't let him in. It's a little abrupt and hard-edged, although after years of hurt and heartache, such walls unfortunately get built and reinforced over time. For a man to prove they are trustworthy and accountable, you need to gift them with opportunities to show you. Being wrapped in steel armor will not allow this to happen.

The healthy and transformational approach to this key element of relationships is to fully embody the Vulnerability Loop as a dance to building both trust and vulnerability at the same time. They are indeed two sides to the same coin.

To embody this Loop, we need to use these layers as intended—to build trust, safety, healthy boundaries, and vulnerability at the same time. As you meet someone, you have all layers up, as you get to know to know them a little and feel safe, you let down the first layer, then observe. If you continue to feel safe, then you allow another to fall away. Then observe. Either he steps up, takes care, becomes The Hero, or not. If you continue to feel safe then you let down another layer, and at any point if you feel unsafe, you address the situation first by taking a step back and pulling up a layer. There's no need to go back to square one, just sidle back up with the last layer you dropped and hold your head high.

There is no need for convoluted conversation or process about this nor do you need to catapult back to full armor protection by ripping back up all layers. Just one layer, and observe, and you continue back and forth in this way until he reveals more of himself to you, and whether or not he can meet your needs for safety, trust and accountability. This process anchors healthy boundaries into the relationship.

Your man will feel the shifts as your Vulnerability Loop moves through different cycles. If you pull up another layer, he will sense this; you do not need to tell him. Remember, his innate and unconscious drive is to get to your innermost center, so when you pull up a layer to keep him at a distance, he will pick up on this and attempt to move closer. In this way, he works out for himself the behavior that has caused the distancing and will attempt to figure it out and adjust that behavior. This enables him to be the hero and for you to build trust. It's genius and it works.

LOVE CHRONICLE #6

Remember my client Gillian? She was recently divorced and had been dating a new man for a year. He was a 'player' in no uncertain terms, and after a month of applying these Codes he turned around and genuinely offered her a full commitment in the direction of marriage and creating a family. True story! What is most interesting about Gillian's story though, is that when she was married, she had an idyllic relationship. Her husband was gorgeous in looks and personality, wealthy and successful, healthy and purposeful. They had a beautiful home, buzzing social life and were part of a meaningful community. Her life looked perfect on the outside, however from the inside, something for Gillian was missing.

Due to this sense of lack she became quite an angry, irritable and often cruel kind of person within the relationship. She could see it brewing in herself, but the character change seemed to have a life of its own, so her husband left her.

What was actually going on for Gillian beneath the surface, was that she never felt seen by her husband. That deep, intimate, soulful connection was missing. There were so many parts of herself that she wanted to express and explore with him, but she couldn't step outside her frustration and instead blamed her husband for her unhappiness within the relationship.

Once the marriage dissolved and she grew interested in The Player a year later, she also started studying with me. It was during her time integrating and working with the Vulnerability Loop that out-of-the-blue, she met a new man. Interestingly, while The Player happened to be doing a full revolution of becoming drawn to Gillian to make a monogamous commitment, this new man seemingly waltzed into her life as though out of a dream! She said me, 'I didn't even know men like this actually existed!' He was that impressive and the attraction so strong, and she felt she could also really open up to him.

And so she broke it off with The Player and decided to give this man a chance. She started to experience the parts of herself that she never got to discover or explore during her marriage. This new man kind of called them all forward and she felt comfortable expressing herself in new and vulnerable ways. She even began to freely express the sides of herself that she assumed were less appealing, sides her ex-husband had demonized, and this was within the first month of dating.

This man fell head-over-heels in love with Gillian and treated her like a goddess. She had found her Level 5 relationship and mastered the Vulnerability Loop so early in the relationship that she could bring all of herself to the commitment. Now, any time you talk to her about her now husband, she melts and blushes and clearly demonstrates that their marriage is full to the brim of juicy relating.

Upon reflection, Gillian said to me one day, 'I wonder what my marriage would have been like if I had this knowledge back then?' And she was right to wonder if things could have turned out differently. This highlights that if you are in a relationship already that is requiring work, I want you to trust that often it's not too late to turn things around. If your feeling is to tend to the relationship rather than end it, then the Love Codes have the capacity to turn it around.

The Vulnerability Loop is a beautiful dance that you and your man can partake in. And he doesn't even need to know that it is happening. As you explore this layered approach, allow him into your circle but don't rush the process. If you find he's not responding to the removal or retrieval of layers, then you'll intuit something's not quite right; that he is perhaps not the man for you. If he's not trustworthy, you'll know because you won't feel safe. There's no need to second guess yourself or work it out, you simply pull up another layer and observe, or if it's become as clear as day that the man is in fact, untrustworthy, then it's time to recognize that this kind of relationship is not for your highest good.

CODE 5 – EVOLUTIONARY SEX

The reason Code 5 is called Evolutionary Sex is because any woman who has had sex knows that there are different kinds of sex. There is sex, and there is Evolutionary Sex.

Most women have had Evolutionary Sex only once or twice in their lifetimes if they are lucky. Most of us have had some great sex but would we consider this Evolutionary Sex? It can be a rarity, and if you've been fortunate to have it, you might look back in hindsight wondering if it was just a fantasy or a lucky streak you were on.

This is the kind of lovemaking where you feel as though the earth has moved beneath you. Your ego dissolves and your body melts into a purity and oneness with All That Is through the earthquake of orgasmic bliss and a profoundly deep connection with your lover. You have merged. There is no separation. Your entire being expands and extends into a delightfully cosmic void of ecstasy and calm. You emerge from this sex feeling satisfied and satiated; settled in the lap of both your souls.

Evolutionary Sex is quite literally, the making of love. Two bodies entwined in an eruption of touch, sensuality, breath, and passion, with loving-locked gazes and the sweet pleasure of skin-on-skin communion. This is how we make love. We are literally drawing in and expressing more love into creation. My interest in intimacy in the form of Evolutionary Sex has led me to research it personally, professionally, and academically. Studied and taught Tantra and explored a variety of approaches to sex and my own sexual nature along the way.

Yet nothing quite compared to what I accidently stumbled across after I had fully integrated the first four Love Codes. Only then did I enter a whole new paradigm of relating with men. I was accessing The Void state effortlessly and frequently. I felt in control and I let the men win. I spent timeless nights and days absorbed in the majesty of my Fairyland. Until one day, I introduced everything about the Love Codes into the bedroom...

The experience was so profound that I knew straight away that this was not to be a once off! That this was the result of all the changes I had made within myself alongside the unshakeable faith and authentic connection I had cultivated with the Divine. It was as though I had transformed in mind, body, and soul to the degree whereby my sex-life had also completely transformed. Lovemaking with my man became an alchemical experience; a sacred space we entered together, and in its wake, we were born anew with a fresh sense of love, devotion and joy bound between us.

This kind of lovemaking is what all men and women crave. It is love-making in the truest sense of the term. It promotes the feeling that when you're engaged in it, from foreplay to the act of sex itself, nothing else in the world exists. It originates from a soul calling to merge with another in love. Through sex, that calling is answered and there's a sense of arriving home, of being touched and carried by the Divine, of releasing all attachments the mind might usually clutch for. All doubt, fear and anxiety cease to exist, and you feel as though you belong, as you are, with *all* that you are.

It may sound too good to be true, that this is the standard of sexual exchange you are worthy of in a relationship with your man. For those of you who have had the pleasure of stumbling across this breath-taking sex, you will know that it is very real and available for women, but the question remains, 'How do we replicate this at will?' And for those of us who haven't had the deep honor of experiencing this type of sex, we still know deep down that it is possible and that there has to be more to it than what we have thus far experienced.

And you would be right. There is a way to replicate the experience at will. The pathway to Evolutionary Sex is through your desire. Before I unpack what this means, I want to qualify that it is essential to first integrate all Love Codes prior to approaching Evolutionary Sex because then you will have the foundations set for your new paradigm of relating to blossom. You will be ready, on all levels, to fearlessly pursue your desire with power and awareness.

Your desires are simply a type of feeling, which as we have touched on, have been sorely distorted by being demonized and emotionalized. And so, with a healthy and authentic desire being the pathway to evolutionary sex; if we try to let our desire lead the way before it has been healed and made whole, we run the risk of inviting trauma, distortion and fear running the show in the bedroom!

When we are able and ready to follow through with the healthy expression of our desires, we enter the realm of Evolutionary Sex. Desire is a particularly interesting feeling state because it is so mercurial; it changes all the time. Depending on our mood, our time of the menstrual cycle, our career peaks and troughs, our creative flow. Bring into the mix that desire by its very nature can only exist when we don't yet have the thing we want and it can be so charged, that we will follow it in any direction.

As modern women we are encouraged to follow our desires. We are taught that desire itself is something to reach for. However, it is much wiser to recognize and value our desire for that which it really is—a signpost along the way to our destination.

Consider your desires as they arise, as signposts along the Yellow Brick Road. Since they express what you want, they have the capacity to lead you towards your ultimate, love-life destination. So, trust them. Lean into them. Yet in the reclamation of these desires as is encouraged these days, know that desire itself will never bring happiness and fulfillment. Desire, in its healthiest application, is a signpost to give you direction.

If you have ever connected to your true desire during sex you will know that it is a wild and unpredictable force. You can find yourself untamed in the throes of carnal passion one minute, only to find yourself craving a snuggle and a kiss-kiss the next. This is one reason why people blatantly choose to be in control rather than open to wherever desire might lead, because of its spontaneous, moment-to-moment nature. It can be thrilling but many are fearful of it. We might fear losing control in general and so many try and tame it.

In addition to encountering fear along the way, on a collective level, our desires have been suppressed and demonized, so we have lost touch with how to open-heartedly ride the waves of desire and allow it to steer us in the direction we want to go. What we tend to do instead is find ourselves in the act and it may be going swimmingly, until the feeling shifts or dissipates completely and instead of going with the shift in desire, we are drawn into our minds thinking, 'Well

I'll do this for now since it seemed to feel good and he liked it,' or we do nothing at all, and suddenly the energy fizzles, the sex is banal and predictable and we've missed the boat on the seas of Evolutionary Sex. Our mind has stepped in, hints of doubt have killed the vibe and we did not grant ourselves the permission to listen to and follow our true desires.

Unfortunately, this chain of events disconnects us from the soul-merging, earth-shaking, ecstatic sex we are longing for. We need to learn to trust our desire, not because it waves the flag for passion and fierce loving but because it is a feeling directly connected to the Divine. When you follow its calling, you are essentially blindfolded. You are in the mystery. The Divine is always couched in the Unknown and the Unseen. You really have no idea where it's going to take you but instinctively, you can trust it will lead you to that place of bliss and soul satisfaction. The time you've spent cultivating your relationship with The Void will show this to be so.

Men already know this about your desire. The freedom-seekers that they are means they've adapted to its unpredictable nature. They like the sense of adventure it brings, the lure of the Unknown. That is why they are drawn to our innate connection to the Divine because it is a natural instinct of theirs to follow it. Our practice lies in continually surrendering and trusting in our desires to take us and our man on a divinely-inspired ride into love and freedom. When you are listening to and following your own desires you will notice that the man you are with will follow suit. It can even transform him from a mediocre lover to Don Juan! (No joke!)

If you are not engaged in Evolutionary Sex with a lover but you would like to, then you need to get intimate with the inner workings of your own desires and bring them to the fore of your relationship. This may take some courage, but the thrill of it is part of the appeal. If we can trust that our desires are inextricably linked as signposts leading us home, then we might begin to listen to them as sacred whisperings. We can shut out the false programming about our authentic desires being irrational, selfish, crazy or unacceptable and honor them as parts of ourselves there to enlighten the way towards our soul destiny.

Remember, your man wants to be The Hero, yet he can't fulfil this promise if he does not know what you desire. He wants to please and pleasure you, make you happy and blissful, feel secure and settled, not solely with the provision of material gains but the kind of security of healthy attachment and devotional love it brings one's heart and soul.

And he wants to do this by satisfying you sexually too because he knows that your sexual openness is a portal for communion with the Divine. It has a nourishing effect on a woman to receive through lovemaking, as it also activates a man to feel empowered to reach his potential. It is a beautiful exchange of the tethering and the awakening of two souls beyond the flesh of body, for both men and women, to cultivate Evolutionary Sex and you can fulfil your role in this by connecting with your deepest desires and allowing yourself to be led by them.

When I say he will follow, I don't just mean in sex, I mean in life. Your sex life could even be a metaphor for the journey. A healthy relationship that allows for your unadulterated feminine desire will feed and strengthen the depth of your connection. It is the key to having that kind of relationship that in our heart of hearts we really want and know is possible. Where, at least in the most intimate spaces we feel we are all of who we are and that our man recognizes and meets us in that wild depth of intimacy and desire.

EVOLUTIONARY RELATIONSHIP WITH THE LOVE CODES

Research indicates that relationships contribute significantly to our happiness and wellbeing. One Harvard study on adult development, which is considered the most extensive study completed on the topic, found that healthy relationships are the most prominent key factor in long lasting happiness.

We do not need statistics to show us this truth; that being nurtured in an unconditionally loving and healthy relationship is bound to bring forth our best selves and improve our life on all levels. That is what we know in our bones and hope to have for ourselves. But as you can see from the ground we have covered in the Love Codes, having an alive, magnetic, dynamic relationship takes dedication and the exploration of areas within yourself, your partner, and your connection. As well as dedication to unravelling eons of negative conditioning to create a version of relationship that is truly fulfilling long-term.

We invest so much energy and money into our careers, personal development, our children, and our passions, yet despite the biological and spiritual need for a loving partnership, we tend to assume that it will just magically work itself out. We may have mastered so many skills in our chosen vocation or refined an art form that brings us joy and satisfaction, but have we taken the time to contemplate the intricacies of our intimate relationships and invest in learning how to make them healthier and more satisfying?

It is my hope with the Love Codes that this transmission guides you on your path of walking that Yellow Brick Road towards your ultimate relationship and brings texture and wisdom to the broad landscape that we travel when we fall in love. There are conscious and unconscious forces at play, divine interventions and connections, there are layers of precious narratives etched in our heart and there is an innocent willingness to enter new terrain in love, romance, passion, and desire. We embrace it all and we get to where we want to go, with these Codes designed to eliminate classic symptoms of heartbreak, sabotage and distorted versions of love, with new re-coded values and beliefs aligned with your heart's true desires.

We cannot sit back idly and wait for Mr. Right to fall into our lap, without also tending to the majesty and richness of our sacred Fairyland, nor avoid getting intimate with our multi-layered, feminine self. We are a gift to man as he is to us, and in doing this work—this inner exploration and healing—we offer ourselves as the most radiant versions of divine love that he craves and wants to worship. Love the journey you are on, whatever stage that may be, and see each stage unfold as an enriching chapter of growth, wisdom, self-discovery, and joy.

Fall in love with your love life and commit to seeing it through to when Evolutionary Relationship becomes the norm. You set the standards; you read those signposts. You are in control and you let him win.

I hope my own dedication and passion for the cause of

supporting and inspiring women on the journey of love has been both educational and comforting for your own personal journey. I feel privileged to walk beside you in complete trust and celebration of the relationship of your dreams to be made manifest and I love watching every woman blossom as the unique, radiant woman that they are, enlightened from the sparks of this process and discovering peace and worthiness in the presence of a Great Man.

Chapter Highlights

Let's recap the Codes:

- ♥ Foundation Code: A woman's role in a relationship is to be the spiritual and emotional guide.

- ♥ Code 1: Attractive Persuasion – A woman is innately connected to the Divine and it is through her that man will find his way home.

- ♥ Code 2: Invisible Influence – I am in control and I let the man win.

- ♥ Code 3: Heartbreak No More – I follow my Yellow Brick Road and re-code unconscious blurts.

- ♥ Code 4: Vulnerability Loop – I dance between vulnerability and trust. If he steps up, I drop another layer.

- ♥ Code 5: Evolutionary Sex – Sacred Evolutionary sex is my birthright. A gift we exchange in trust, desire, devotion and passionate love.

5

EXTENDED RESOURCES

THE VOID PRACTICE

I highly recommend that you do this practice by using the recorded guidance from me by accessing the following link:

https://belindabailey.com.au/the-void-practice/

It is also possible, however not nearly as powerful to do it by reading it first and taking yourself through the process.

Find a time and space where you won't be interrupted. Put everything aside and get into a comfortable sitting position. Close your eyes.

Notice the color of your eyelids—the dark, black nothingness. Tune into the sensation of your body and its aliveness. Whatever you hear, smell, sense, is all perfect. Allow your attention to shift inwards.

Scan and explore the deeper, darker landscape of your body while observing your breath to rise and fall. Notice the natural rhythm of your breath and the space and stillness between inhalation and exhalation.

Now focus on the non-moving state of stillness that sits behind the motion of the breath. Identify your 'self' as that stillness. Observe and be at one with it. Your breath is layered upon it and you can rest in the lap of its calm expansiveness.

In a moment, I want you to slowly open your eyes. To do so with a delicate connection and awareness of the depth of space you've been meditating on. One, two, three, open. You may feel expanded and light. You have accessed The Void and brought it into your awareness. Notice how vast it is and how easy it is to connect with. You can revisit it any time using this simple technique.

THE LOVE CODES – EXTENDED TRAINING

Now that you have the Love Codes you may feel ready to dive deeper into an accelerated, transformational process to support you on your journey towards manifesting a Level 5 Evolutionary Relationship. This is what my extended training is designed for. Here is an outline of the themes covered in the training, which you can view in full via the website:

www.belindabailey.com.au/the-love-codes-program/

The New Paradigm Relationship

We have touched on this foundational element in this book and yet there is more to explore in terms of understanding and embodying a woman's role and the power she holds in a relationship as The Guide. We look at real life situations to apply this wisdom and erase old programs that may be blocking your neural pathways in stepping fully into this role, unencumbered.

We continue to explore The Void, strengthening our personal communion with it and unpack this concept further so that it is anchored as an everyday force you can tap into. I will teach you two more Void practices to assist your development. One is an expression practice using your speech. The other is designed by Dr Saida Desilet, who has developed especially for the Love Codes, an embodiment practice to align you directly with The Void.

Fulfilling Your Calling and Purpose Through Relationship

I introduce this concept based on the common obstacle women face when falling in love with a man and then losing touch with themselves and their highest calling. Your relationship has the potential to further actualize and enhance your life purpose, not distract you or drain your energy. In this module we look at creating a relationship that is in alignment with your purpose, and that as the relationship grows, so too does it nourish your passions, career, and soul purpose.

Evolutionary Relationship:
The Automated Organism for Evolution

In my perspective, this is one of the most exciting parts of an Evolutionary Relationship because it places relationships at the center of our world as a tool for evolution and growth. Due to the type of relationship you are bound to attract using The Map, whereby you and your man are both in your power, you are inadvertently fulfilling a big part of the collective purpose of humanity. When two people are dedicated to Divine Union, they are assisting the collective to rise into higher states of unconditional love, harmony, trust, and joy. Through the relationship's symbiosis, you are naturally feeding off each other's growth and being propelled to live as your true self, on purpose and in service of the greater good. Your relationship becomes a beacon for humanity.

The Un-Demonization of Feelings

With this module I conduct a complete re-programming of your connection to your feelings so that you are no longer governed by your emotional self but instead, conversing with your divine guidance and following your intuition. This becomes effortless when we have removed the influence of trauma, distortions or toxicity that may be influencing your ability to accurately interpret your feeling nature. You will find sweet relief in not having to question or filter yourself in the presence of man.

Anchoring His Attention To You

If you have ever felt jealousy or uncertainty with a man, this module will help you turn that around and become secure in the knowledge that his attention is anchored to you. With this in place, external concerns won't even enter your mind anymore. It provides you with a sense of freedom and security within yourself without having to seek out validation from him.

Your Untouched Attraction Power

This is a personal favorite. The golden shadow! We re-code your emotions so that what used to be your 'real' emotional self that 'scared' men away, becomes the actual things that attracts them to you. This is what I love about this work—you don't have to stop being anything. This module simply aligns you to a healthy emotional intelligence within yourself which, in turn, attracts the right kind of man and relationship for you. This translates to anything you considered as anger or fear arising in you to become transformed into that which attracts and draws a man closer to you.

Inspired Commitment

A popular secret among clients, the Commitment Creating Secret, delves into the psychology of commitment for men, to learn how to *inspire* rather than force a commitment from them. Even though their psychology around commitment is very different to women, it does not mean they don't want it. They absolutely do and this part of the training will support you in approaching this aspect of your relationship.

The Language of Influence Package

This ties in and expands upon the Invisible Influence Code. This package will teach you how to feel confident in your innate language of communication with a man. We look at the feminine language as opposed to a more masculine way of expressing ourselves, which has held a strong influence. Having this tool under your belt will increase the polarity and tension within your dynamic in an effortless manner, creating beautiful points of intimacy and connection.

We also look at how expectation is *not* a dirty word. How many times have you heard: 'Don't have any expectations!' Or you have said, 'I don't have any expectations!' Dropping expectations altogether has the effect of turning great men into jerks. You actually benefit from having expectations; they create standards. We unpack the importance of expectations in this package also.

The Win-Win Formula

This module solidifies how to be in control and let the man win. What I love about this formula is that it allows you to trust that butterfly-in-the-stomach experience time and time again with your man, who demonstrates himself to be a very positive match for you because he is trustworthy, and you always feel safe.

If you've found that you have had such damaging experiences with men that has led you to be unable to trust again, then this module supports you to heal and recover from that cycle as a sure-fire way to become vulnerable again in a safe way to invite in love from a man you can trust.

Recoding the Yellow Brick Road

This process is an extension of our path towards a Level 5 Relationship where we re-code our attraction pathways so that what we attract aligns with our Yellow Brick Road. We learn how to quickly recognize when a man might be veering us off track, which enables you to stop wasting time and energy in relationships that are not for your highest good.

With the new Codes, we get a head-start towards our end goal also, which means that every time you start a new relationship you can trust it is the best possible starting point for you. This ensures you are constantly moving towards your dream relationship, and eliminates doubt.

Complete Recoding of Poison Blurts

As promised, we eliminate those pesky diversions for good with a complete reprogramming of your unconscious belief systems. This forms quite a large part of the training as we exhaust all areas of the unconscious mind, but it is an extremely wise and rewarding investment for the future of your love life.

Once you have completely re-coded Poison Blurts, you will feel innately connected to your desired outcome on a quantum level. This process is life-changing and guarantees a complete upgrade of the men you start attracting into your life. Or the behavior that your current man displays.

Calibrating Your Inner-Compass

In this module we build upon what we have learnt with The Vulnerability Loop, with this organic process of opening and closing your inner-most self without pulling out entirely. We fully integrate the layered approach to trust and vulnerability so you have a strong internal compass to always guide you.

The Power of an Elegant Exit

Lastly, even though no one wants to think about ending a relationship, it does occur and this resource will provide you with approaches you can use to leave a relationship that honors both yourself and the man, without drama. This is an invaluable tool to have, and ensures you aren't wasting time on a dead-end relationship simply because you can't find a way out. Heartache and pain are replaced with grace and conscious uncoupling, which puts you in good stead for the next part of your love life journey.

RESOURCES

Below is a list of links to resources that have been mentioned in the book as a gift to help you on your journey to discovering your own relating patterns that are standing in your way. These resources will also provide you with support to apply the Love Codes and start having a healthy, Evolutionary Relationship.

Love Life Spectrum Profiling

Void practice

The Poison Blurt process

https://belindabailey.com.au/the-love-codes-resources/

WORK WITH BELINDA BAILEY AND THE LOVE CODES

Website

https://belindabailey.com.au

Get to Know the Love Codes Audio Training

https://belindabailey.com.au/get-to-know-the-love-codes/

Facebook

https://www.facebook.com/juicyrelating

The Love Codes Full Training Program

https://belindabailey.com.au/the-love-codes-program/

Instagram

https://www.instagram.com/belindabailey_relationships/

Email

assist@belindabailey.com

AUTHOR
CONTACT PAGE

Email
belle@belindabailey.com

Website
https://belindabailey.com.au/

Instagram
https://www.instagram.com/belindabailey_relationships/

Facebook
https://www.facebook.com/juicyrelating/

Did you enjoy reading this book?

Please take a few moments to post a positive review on Amazon - tell us what you loved about the book so that others can benefit from your experience of it and hopefully enjoy it too. Thank you!

REFERENCES

London School of Economics research on how relationships affect happiness
www.lse.ac.uk/News/Latest-news-from-LSE/2016/12-December-2016-1/Relationships-and-happiness)

The Dalai Lama – Vancouver Peace Summit
https://dalailamacenter.org/blog-post/western-women-can-come-rescue-world

Dr Joe Dispenza and his mammoth contribution to Quantum Healing and Human Transformation
https://drjoedispenza.com/

The Good News Guide – for support for this book as well as quality guidance in the area of Human Transformation
https://www.lisawinneke.com/thegoodnewsguide

EXTRA READING

Further reading and inspiration for this book.

Becoming Supernatural by Dr Joe Dispenza

The Hero with a Thousand Faces by Joseph Campbell

Whispers in the Wind by John Grinder

Raising Boys by Steven Biddulph

God Wears Lipstick by Karen Berg

Mating in Captivity by Esther Perel

Desire by Dr Saida Desilets

ABOUT THE AUTHOR

Belinda is a consultant, educator, and facilitator on the frontiers of evolutionary love relationships. Her wisdom and skills have been honed over decades, culminating in events, workshops and private coaching sessions for clients who are ready and willing to revolutionize their love-life.

Her work is infused with compassion and wisdom. As a devoted mother and wife, Belinda has walked many paths towards a soul aligned partnership and lifestyle based on deep love, intimacy, harmony, and joy. Drawing from her studies alongside her lived experience of personal and spiritual development, she now supports women on their own journey creating lasting, fulfilling relationships.

Contagiously passionate about human transformation and a big believer in the power of change, Belinda's commitment to her audience lies in ensuring that the experience of how to love and be loved is a fully attainable and satisfying quest, one that we are all naturally geared for.

Through application of Transpersonal Psychology and Neural and Behavioral Change techniques, as well as growing education in cutting-edge Quantum psychology, meditation and epigenetics, working with Belinda is a testament to the power of human potential.

Her steadfast trust in the process of neurological malleability, matched with her wise stewardship in the face of any obstacles standing in the way of true love, has gained her recognition among many as a leader in the field of conscious relating.

Belinda's flagship program, The Love Codes, is her most popular program to date after more than 20 years of contributing to educational seminars in her field. She offers private consultation for groups, individuals, and couples worldwide and continues to deliver sold-out events.

Every day, Belinda's gratitude for the depth of love and soul-fueled companionship she shares with her husband on the parenting journey with their gorgeous son, reminds her of the immense value of the wellspring of her work and its ongoing rewards in her own life and the life of many others.

ACKNOWLEDGMENTS

Reading the acknowledgments page of a book always seemed like an overzealous Oscar speech to me. Until I actually wrote a book! And then I realized just how much time and energy it takes to bring to life. And with this as the case, it requires so much support and encouragement from those around us. And so, if you will allow me the indulgence of my 'Oscar moment' there are many people who have helped to birth this beautiful book.

Starting with my ex-husband, Mardi, who, loved me with all his heart and did his very best to create a happy marriage and in all of his and my own short comings, inadvertently created the fertile breeding ground for this work. Thank you for always doing your best. I am sorry that I didn't have this wisdom sooner and am so grateful to have your friendship still and that you, too, have created a loving family with a beautiful partner.

All my past partners and lovers who (without always knowing it) were (usually) willing experiments for all of the wisdom held in this book.

Nell and Ian Clarke who nurtured me through the breakdown of my first marriage and always believed in me. Nell, you are my fairy godmother.

To my actual mum and dad. I know it won't be easy for them to read parts of this book but without the journey we have had, I would not have been able to learn what I've learned.

And to my mum especially who has willingly grown and

healed from this too and now become a wonderful ally for me and my family and support for me in my own journey of motherhood.

As well as my sister Rachael who has been and continues to be an ally on the entire journey. The older I get, the more I understand how having a sister is one of the greatest blessings.

To my own coaches, Perry Mardon, who reminded me of the big work that I am here to do and that I *have to do it*. And Millie Swan who literally saved me from my self by embodying true divine maternal love. Fierce, unapologetic, and healing.

To all of the teachers who have taught me and guided me in deepening my understanding and passion for all things to do with human potential and transpersonal psychology. Rapahel Locke, Martin Peake, John Grinder, Jules and Chris Collingwood and the revolutionary Dr Joe Dispenza.

My Queens Council. Devashi Shakti, Lauren Woodman, Emma Kenyon and Marina Perry, and Amanda Leigh Walker who have been the absolute epitome of strength in the feminine, setting the bar high and holding me in the greatest vision when I couldn't.

Special thanks to Russel Price who supported me deeply in the beginnings of this work and inspired me with his own fascination of relationships and afforded me the phrase of the Love Codes Mantra: 'I am in control by letting the man win.'

All my beta readers who gave useful and supportive feedback and encouragement. Dr Saida Desilet, Millie Swan, Petra Brzovic, Rachel Heller. And especially Amanda Leigh Walker who basically helped me to rewrite the whole book!

Lisa Winneke of the *Good News Guide*, for giving me a

platform for the voice of this work, when I was unable to run my own programs due to motherhood and lockdown. Thank you for keeping the voice of the Love Codes alive during this time.

Charlotte Myers, for your beautiful and poignant artistry in helping to write this book. Your deep understanding of this work, together with your divine gift of writing, has made this book what it is.

The team at Inspire Media – Amanda Spedding my editor, Sophie White my book designer and of course Julie Postance my book publishing consultant who, as well as having been my savior in guiding me every step of the way to bring this book to life, is also a special and beautiful human being that I absolutely love working with. Who has made it feel possible to even write another book!

Martia Mckinnon, my dearest friend. Your love, support, friendship is so deep and great. Always the voice of reason to remind me to slow down and take a breath so that I can do my best work.

I've said it already and I'll say it again. Warwick, my husband, for allowing me so much time and space to do this work and to rest and recuperate. For holding the fort so often so that I can receive the guidance that comes to me in times of solitude. And for believing in this work so much that you do all that you do with love and grace. I am so deeply blessed.

And of course Caleb, our son, for making my life an absolute joy and feeling like I am the cat that got the cream. In amongst all of the things I do and love, the thing that I love most of all in life is being your mummy. x